D1546324

THE ROADMAP *to* DIVINE DIRECTION

FINDING GOD'S WILL FOR EVERY SITUATION

DESTINY IMAGE BOOKS BY BRENDA KUNNEMAN

Decoding Hell's Propaganda

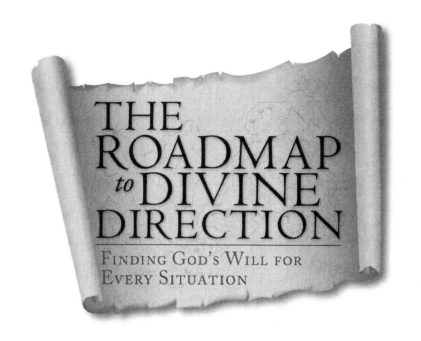

THE
ROADMAP
to DIVINE
DIRECTION

FINDING GOD'S WILL FOR
EVERY SITUATION

BRENDA KUNNEMAN

DESTINY IMAGE® PUBLISHERS, INC.

P.O. Box 310, Shippensburg, PA 17257-0310

"Promoting Inspired Lives."

This book and all other Destiny Image, Revival Press, MercyPlace, Fresh Bread, Destiny Image Fiction, and Treasure House books are available at Christian bookstores and distributors worldwide.

For a U.S. bookstore nearest you, call 1-800-722-6774.

For more information on foreign distributors, call 717-532-3040.

Reach us on the Internet: www.destinyimage.com.

ISBN 13 TP: 978-0-7684-3964-9

ISBN 13 Ebook: 978-0-7684-8936-1

For Worldwide Distribution, Printed in the U.S.A.

1 2 3 4 5 6 7 8 9 10 11 / 13 12 11

DEDICATION

This book is dedicated to all the wonderful family of Lord of Hosts Church in Omaha, Nebraska, who are always so supportive toward me and who work hard to embrace God's perfect will in their lives.

CONTENTS

INTRODUCTION

If you have served God for any length of time, you have probably sought His will for your life on countless occasions. Some such occasions, if you were to be honest with yourself, likely included what perhaps felt like a guessing game.

Having spent most of my adult life in some ministry capacity, I have been on numerous quests to find God's will for not only the things that pertain to me, but also to help countless others locate the will of God. Those quests include everything from simple parenting issues, to the larger life-long decisions, ministry plans, relationships and even just the things that pertain to everyday life. I have had some situations where I felt like finding God's will was not much more than that dreaded guessing game. Other times I came away from it and felt like I totally missed God's direction! Then I have had those amazing times when no one's opinion, no challenge or storm could sway what I believe to be God's will, and I stepped right into it in a supernatural way.

Regardless of which scenario presents itself, one of the worst feelings for any believer is to feel that they are missing God's will in some capacity. Whether that feeling occurred because of a deliberate wrong choice or simply because you are unsure of yourself, no one wants to question whether or not they are in God's perfect will. Beyond that, an even worse feeling is knowing that you missed or even ignored God's will and now you are living with trying to repair the present circumstances that came as a result. No one wants to be out of God's will, for to be out of His will is to miss His greatest blessings.

In some cases, people work so hard to find God's will they have become obsessed and excessive in their attempt to find it. They often begin looking in all the wrong places or begin looking at unreliable resources. Some believers have even become delusional by searching out strange occurrences that they believe are God's guiding light to them. As a result, some have even opened themselves up to evil spirits. Others, work so hard trying to figure out God's will, they exhaust themselves into frustration. They can't find any peace where God is leading them and will continue to lead them.

What we need to know is that learning to successfully find and follow God's will is the lifeblood to being a flourishing Christian. You simply cannot succeed without it. The truth is that many of us don't spend the necessary time to developing expertise in this area. Therefore, we resign our lives to that guessing game that we desperately wish we knew how to avoid.

This doesn't have to be your story. There is a roadmap to finding God's divine direction in every circumstance of life. Truthfully, no one can locate that roadmap for you, even though that might feel a lot easier at times! No, there is a roadmap God wants to lead you on today, but you have to know how to read the map.

I believe this book will set you on a confident course to finding God's will, not only for your destiny in life, but also for everyday life. Even in some of those trickier circumstances when you just don't seem to know what to do, you can follow God's will with confidence if you put certain things to practice. From everything to using Scripture for finding God's will or hearing God through circumstances, other people or even His voice within, you can learn to find the perfect will of God in every situation.

When presented with common questions such as, "Should I take that job?" or "Should I buy that house?" or even "Should I take that medicine?" God wants you to rise above these things and learn how to peacefully find His divine direction.

The Bible says that wisdom is crying aloud in the streets! (see Prov 8:1-3) In other words, God's will and all wise answers are not hard to locate. It's there in front of everyone of us, but we have to know where and how to look.

Before you read the principles in this book, let's begin with prayer. I am believing a supernatural event will take place within you that will cause you to receive divine direction in a unique way. Let's trust God together that you will stand confidently in finding His will for every situation.

Dear Heavenly Father,

I know that you have a plan for my life and a word of direction for everything I face. My heart's desire is to follow you in every circumstance. Lord, I desire to know your will for everything that pertains to my life.

I ask that you would reveal my purpose and destiny. I also ask you to show me your direction concerning _____ (name a particular situation). As you make known your perfect will for me, Lord, I commit myself to you in total obedience. I choose to follow your will even during those times when it might feel difficult to do so. I also make a fresh commitment of obedience to your will that is found in the Bible. Give me the strength to do all that you have asked of me. I believe today that I will not miss Your will for me in any area and I declare that divine direction and revelation are manifesting upon me today! In Jesus' Name, Amen!

I have no doubt that by the time you are finished reading this book, that you will have received divine direction regarding some things that have been important to you. I trust that you will be more confident about what to do. Rest assured today that God's roadmap of divine direction, even if your situation is challenging, is already working in your life and you are going to know His perfect will in every thing you face. It's time…yes, it's time to end that guessing game!

Chapter One

YOU CAN KNOW GOD'S WILL

Wherefore be ye not unwise, but understanding what the will of the Lord is (Ephesians 5:17).

I am not great at puzzles. Especially the 5000-piece puzzles that almost require a microscope to see the pieces. Actually, no kind of puzzle is my bag. Not word-find, Rubik's cube, crosswords, jigsaw puzzles—none of them. I have tried them all, but truthfully, I struggle with every puzzle I attempt. Of course, I tackle each new puzzle with determined expectancy and fervor, but each endeavor mostly turns out the same. I grab the puzzle pieces or paper and pencil ready to conquer the thing with my strategy before me, but it's always the same story. Either I can't solve it at all, or it takes me what feels like centuries to complete, so I typically lose interest.

I think my problem is I just try too hard. I look and examine every piece in detail. With those jigsaw puzzles, I just stare at the pieces and try to see where they would fit best. I look and look, comparing the print and the shapes. Suddenly, it happens! My moment of revelation has come. I grab a puzzle piece and excitedly plant it in the spot where I know it's going to fit! What? It doesn't fit? Yep, that's my real story on puzzle work. The harder I try, the worse I feel when I can't solve the puzzle.

Of course, my husband and youngest son are puzzle masters. It frustrates me, actually. You know the family scene. We pop the popcorn, pour the soda, spread the puzzle across the table, and gather around. Piece after piece, they are putting them in place. I look and look so long that when I finally come upon a fit, the family, sensing my despair, breaks into comments of encouragement for me. I have even received puzzle mentoring from them when they begin to feel bad that I can't find a fit. Yes, they stop working on their own puzzle work and start helping me! It's all wrong you know. You could say I am not a puzzle person.

The only thing I can figure out on why puzzles are so challenging for me is I make them too hard in my own mind and want them completed in a very short time. I work myself up, get a plan and strategy, and look at the thing with a determination to conquer it faster than anyone else, but then I wind up struggling. In the end, I would rather someone else do it so I can walk up to the completed project and stand in awe of the accomplishment when it's over. I want to see it when it's done and ignore the steps in between. I just like to enjoy the grand and glorious moment, and I want it all to happen in one instant.

I do believe this is how many people treat God's will and plan for their lives. They make it too hard in their own minds, and as a result, they don't want to walk it out, or they simply walk it out with too much skepticism. They want the result without the process. Truthfully, the will of God in our lives is like a puzzle.

Ephesians 5:17 says, *"Wherefore be ye not unwise, but understanding what the will of the Lord is."* At first glance, we could take this verse to mean that we had better have God's will down pat and be able to recite it exactly, assuming that is what it means to "understand His will." Really the word understanding in this verse, according to Strong's Concordance, means "to put together." It is basically indicating that we "put together" our ability to comprehend or understand piece by piece. What we need to realize is that putting anything together is a process, and finding God's will in anything is no different. It typically isn't a brief momentary event but something that is developed through time—step by step.

Have you ever purchased one of those put-it-together-yourself pieces of furniture? You don't see the finished product all in one step. It comes through many steps, and sometimes those steps include a little trial and error! Usually the package includes some arduous instructions that don't appear very clear at first glance. But you pick up the parts, put them back down, then read the instructions again and again. You examine the diagrams. Sometimes you make mistakes and have to retrace a few steps. Sure, there is some trial and even error, but as you stay with it, you finally end up with the intended finished product.

The Bible is very clear on this point, as the familiar verse says in Psalm 37:23-24:

> *The steps of a good man are ordered by the Lord: and*
> *He delighteth in his way. Though he fall, he shall not*

*be utterly cast down: for the Lord upholdeth him with
His hand.*

Notice it says *steps*. If you want your life to be divinely directed, you must be willing to accept the fact that it will occur in the process of taking individual steps in which you may not see the big picture. You may even feel like some pieces are missing. Then eventually, when all the pieces are put together, God's plan will become clear to you.

So when the Bible tells us not to be unwise, but understanding what the will of the Lord is, it is saying that we need to be wise enough to keep putting together the pieces of the puzzle until the whole thing becomes clear.

Sometimes we get the idea that we should be able to instantly recognize God's will for our every move all the time and be able to determine our course of action for the next five years into the future. Preachers especially feel this pressure because everyone expects them to be able to hear from God regarding everything without a problem.

Sure, you can and often will get some basic images of God's future plan this way. However, the Lord is using those moments when you think you have lost your way to develop you into who you are meant to become. Sometimes God will purposely keep certain parts of the plan hidden from your eyes so you will walk forward with faith and trust in Him. That means you don't have to feel the pressure to explain to everyone what step in God's will you are walking out right now.

Truth is, sometimes we just don't know. However, the fact remains that sometimes we don't need to know, and let's go one further—sometimes you don't want to know! God won't tell you everything because if He did, you wouldn't be able to handle it. Just realize, when you think the "puzzle piece" you need is lost, you may not realize that the power of the Holy Spirit is planting it in front of you, and you are following it without realizing it.

Knowing the will of God, whether for the big picture of your life or just one specific situation or decision, becomes easier when you understand that God operates step by step and that He allows many things to remain a mystery while you are walking them out by faith.

When the Lord first prophesied about the coming Messiah, in the Garden of Eden in Genesis 3:15, it was only the first piece. Through the years, God kept raising up prophets and chosen people to reveal other pieces. By the time Jesus was born, all the pieces had nearly come together, but God purposely left a few out until just the right time. Those missing pieces ended up keeping the demons of hell totally in the dark. They couldn't figure out the big picture.

First Corinthians 2:7-8 says:

> *But we speak the wisdom of God in a mystery, even the hidden wisdom, which God ordained before the world unto our glory: which none of the princes of this world knew: for had they known it, they would not have crucified the Lord of glory.*

God in His wisdom held back just the right pieces until the perfect time so the devil wouldn't know everything God was up to. Even the demons in their ignorance became obvious pieces of the picture themselves when Jesus arose from the grave and embarrassed them (see Col. 2:15). This should make us even more thankful that God doesn't reveal everything at the time.

God might be holding back some of the pieces in your life right now on purpose. But if you are faithfully committed to Him, the Lord will circle you right back around and keep you on track. Your steps will be divinely ordered, and it will be done without the wrong interference from yourself, other people, or even the devil. Thank God for His wisdom.

If we serve God wholeheartedly and with humility every day, we will eventually "put together" the puzzle of our lives that the Lord has perfectly designed according to His divine will. We won't miss the big picture of the finished "puzzle" if we keep working the "pieces" with God.

Remember, it's piece by piece or step by step. Right now there are countless missing pieces and many things may not look complete to you, but there is a big picture in the making, and all you have to do is focus on today's piece. It's through that process that you will eventually put all the pieces of God's will for your life together, and the entire plan will come together. Sometimes, you will attempt to fit the wrong piece into place, but if you stay close to God, you will find yourself ultimately putting the right pieces together.

YOU NEVER HAVE TO MISS GOD'S WILL

You are probably following God's perfect will for your life better than you can see. There are some key directives in the famous verses of Psalm 37:23-24 that will help you know why you won't miss God's will for you. Let's look at the verses again.

> *The steps of a good man are ordered by the Lord: and He delighteth in his way. Though he fall, he shall not be utterly cast down: for the Lord upholdeth him with His hand.*

Not only is the passage telling us that God orders our way through steps of faith, but also that when we do make mistakes, we literally can't be permanently thrown off the right track because the Lord's hand is there to keep us on target. God is ordering our steps even when we feel like we've lost our direction and don't know what is going on.

When you feel like you can't "find the right piece" of the puzzle, you can rest assured that God will keep you going in the right direction.

That said, there is still something we need to do here that is found in a key phrase in these verses. Notice it says, "and He delighteth in his way." The Amplified Bible shows it more clearly. It says:

> *The steps of a [good] man are directed and established by the Lord when He delights in his way [and He busies Himself with his every step]. Though he falls, he shall not be utterly cast down, for the Lord grasps his hand in support and upholds him.*

Really, this is a pretty simple, but it's still a breakthrough revelation for ensuring we never miss the will of God. All we need to do is be busy about pleasing the Lord. That means we obey the Bible, even the parts we don't like as much! It means we pray and stay in close fellowship with God. We live our lives pursuing God with all our effort. This type of lifestyle, according to these verses, ensures that we will never miss the perfect will of God for our lives.

Really? You might be saying, Is that even possible? Yes, that is exactly what the Bible is saying here. It doesn't say you have to acknowledge that you know every detail of God's will for you. It just tells you to press in to God and rest assured He will handle it from there. You just press in step by step and piece by piece every day with God, doing what is right and honorable to Him, and let God unfold the rest.

THE UNWANTED BUILDING

When we started our church in 1997, we rented a very small retail space of about 3,800 square feet in a rather rundown shopping plaza. There was nothing complimentary about it. The carpet was horrible. The outside of the building was dated and full of flaws. The roof leaked—a lot. However, the rent was cheap, and cheap is good! We fixed up the place the best we could with some paint and a little hard work. Yes, Lord of Hosts Church was born in a very humble manger.

The lease we signed was only for a few short months because we were convinced we wouldn't be there long. We didn't want to be there because the place wasn't very nice, so in our minds it was a temporary start to a brighter future in the ministry someday.

However, what we thought was about to be an earlier-than-expected departure ended up being an expansion of space and a new lease. We were nearly asked to leave the shopping center when our drums were too loud for the other businesses open on Sundays. However, the landlord was compassionate, and rather than push the church out of the center altogether, they allowed us to rent another space farther away from other tenants.

It was bigger and cost a little more, and again, the place was awful. We had to fix it up again, but this one also needed some construction. Walls were broken down, carpet was torn up, wires were hanging everywhere, and it smelled horrible. But taking this space was the only visible step we had in front of us, so we agreed to yet another short, "temporary" lease. We kept the lease short because we were determined that even though we would fix it up for now, we didn't want to be in that center for long. We continued looking at every possible option to move the church elsewhere.

Fast forward ten years. By that time, we had added numerous bay spaces, given up a few, gained them back, and turned all our little spaces into one expansive facility until it was the largest single tenant space in the entire building. We've often joked that our church is like a set of toy Legos. You add a piece here and there and then remove a few and add them back until you get something recognizable.

Yes, nearly 14 years later at the time of this writing, we are still in that unwanted building that was "temporary"! We have made a permanent imprint on it, and that ugly duckling space is now a beautiful facility inside. It has hosted some of the most recognized, quality ministries worldwide and is now fully equipped for television.

Now here is the part I want you to see. We prayed count-less times about leaving, but one step at a time, the building we tried to leave kept growing up around us! While we kept looking for greener grass someplace else, we were finally forced to acknowledge that in some way this building held a key piece to God's prophetic plan for our ministry. The thing just wouldn't go away! In fact, we have talked and written about it countless times, and it continues to be the subject of great sermon material.

You see, we can often make the puzzle harder than it needs to be. Sometimes the obvious step is the very thing we are walking out right now. Too often it's the only obvious thing in front of us. It's a good thing the Lord didn't tell us on the day we signed our first lease that we would be there for the next 14 years of our ministry. I think if He did, we would have been tempted to give up the ministry!

The steps you are walking out right now may not be what you planned for, and your situation may not look at all like what you originally envisioned, but the result is the same. God is doing something powerful through you because you stayed pressed in to Him!

Perhaps in your quest to follow God's will, you've made some wrong decisions or even terrible mistakes, and now you are living in the consequences. If so, return to God again! If you return to God, He will return to you (see Mal. 3:7). You might have put yourself on a cumbersome detour due to some bad decisions. Nevertheless, get back into delight-ing in the Lord and keep taking the steps in front of you by faith today.

The Spirit of God has an incredible way of bringing you back around to where you need to be, full circle. Don't worry about what each piece looks like right now. Sure, you may wish you were somewhere else, in another city, in a different house or—in our case—in another building! But, if you press in to Him, rest assured the Lord will set you on His anointed path. You won't miss it!

Chapter Two

LEARNING TO LISTEN
TO YOUR HEART

...but the Lord was not in the fire... (1 Kings 19:12).

Often when it comes to finding God's will in a situation, we aren't certain where we should begin looking for His voice. As a result, we sometimes go back and forth between various emotional feelings about something or instead we try our best to take the most reasonable and logical approach.

Both emotions and logic can and will play a part in decision making, so before we talk about where to begin looking for the voice of the Lord, let's discuss briefly how both emotions and logic affect our ability to hear the Lord.

A lot could be said about emotions. We all have them, and we have all experienced times when they have gotten out of hand. Wrongly followed, emotions can either prevent us from accepting God's blessings or pressure us into things we later wish we would have avoided. A vast amount of credit card debt is created simply because of undisciplined emotions!

Actually, emotions are from God, and they are meant to be used to help us relate to Him on a personal level. They help us express an appreciation for righteousness or a hatred of sin. They help us form likes and dislikes. They also allow us to express the joy and love of the Lord. However, we can't rely solely on emotions when it comes to making big decisions. We shouldn't depend on them to find the will of God because emotions are ever changing, sometimes from day to day or even hour to hour! Emotions can feel good about something just because it is a bright sunny day or bad about something because the sky is overcast.

God doesn't rely on these kinds of constantly changing emotions. When He created humanity, He did it through a well-thought-out decision. He thought all the way through eternity and was fully aware of the costs involved. Even in spite of the evils in the world, God has never given up on humanity. He has remained constant in His decision of creating the world, even when some of the people He lovingly created have rejected Him.

The other key part of our mental psyche is logic and human reasoning. While some people tend to fall on emotions to make decisions, others tend to rely on logic. Just like emotions, logic and intellect are also from God. This is where we get the phrase, "Use your brain!" Logic can help us make sensible choices as we weigh out the facts or pros and cons in any situation. Logic can help us make wise decisions and help us see the benefits of serving God. Logic helps us understand that eating vegetables is a better decision than eating a bag of potato chips.

Just like emotions, however, logic cannot be our sole method of finding the will of God. This is because God doesn't operate by the limited power of human logic; He operates by faith! When over-emphasized, our logical intellect becomes one of the greatest enemies of the anointing. This is because it can reason us out of God's promises and blessings. God's blessings come because of our faith and ability to believe them, even when all the natural facts don't line up.

We definitely need to use our God-given ability for logical reason; however, we can look so excessively hard at all the facts and explanations until we reason the miraculous and unexplainable things of God right out of our lives. Many people miss out on some incredible miracles because of logic. They are more apt to question the legitimacy of a miracle than they are willing to look for reasons to believe in it. They are stuck in their heads, but the supernatural is not limited by the boundaries of mental logic.

Scientists have spent decades using logic to try to explain why it is impossible for the parting of the Red Sea or the story of Noah's Ark to have happened. Of course, by natural, scientific methods, these things are impossible. These occurrences may not be remotely explainable, but God isn't bound to the facts and laws of physical science. You can't figure Him out that way! Often you just have to believe Him when nothing adds up.

Had God only looked at logic when it came to creating us, the negatives could have easily made it look like He should avoid creating humanity. To logical thinking, the negatives could have outweighed the positives. But God did not make His decision based on logic—and we are all thankful for that.

So, although we can see that both emotions and logic will take part in our decision making, they aren't fully dependable when it comes to finding God's will for us. They are only there to aid us.

Where we need to first look for the answers we seek is deep down in our spirits where the Holy Spirit dwells. We need to learn how to rely on our inner person, where the Spirit of God is, and then let things like emotions and intellect come alongside to aid and confirm what our spirit is telling us.

Not long after we started our church, a couple from out of state who had been friends of our family for quite a few years took an interest to moving to Omaha to be a part of our newly formed church. The man had been a friend of my husband since we were first married, and they had a great friendship surrounding the things of the Lord. After this man and his wife were married, she also really connected with us, and we further built on our friendship. Shortly after the church took off, they decided to come out for a visit, trying to decide if they should move to Omaha to be a part of the church.

Of course, at the time, our church was still in its most humble beginnings, so for them to move here would have been a step of faith. The logical question was, "What would they be coming here for?" There were countless more impressive and well-established churches right where they lived.

Yes, those were the days when our church was tiny and clad with horrible blue shag carpet and hand-me-down orange upholstered pews. There was no true platform, just a "stage area." So our friends certainly weren't moving here because they were impressed by the ministerial frills and lights! Plus, they didn't have any job security in coming. They would arrive and have to look for work because we didn't have any openings for jobs.

During their process of deciding what to do, we had many talks and discussions together. Of course our emotional side wanted them to come! They could have also made their final decision based on normal emotions stemming from our mutual friendship.

We resisted the urge to influence them in any way. We didn't want them to make an emotional decision because of our own excitement, nor did we want them to just look at all the logical reasoning that might talk them out of it. Too much influence from us as the pastors would have only increased the pressure for all of us to keep the "it's the will of God feeling" when challenging times arose.

In every situation, challenging times will arise, even when we are in God's will. Yet, when people hear from God inside themselves, without all kinds of people or other outside sources influencing what they are sensing, it builds their faith to remain steadfast even in tough times. They also become more confident that they can hear from God for themselves during those times when outside input simply isn't available.

When you learn to hear God from inside your spirit, where the Holy Spirit dwells, you will also find that not only do you become more confident of His voice but that you are less influenced by the wrong things.

This, of course, doesn't mean that we don't need the input of others. We absolutely need people to speak into our lives, and we will discuss how to accurately listen to the will of God through others in a later chapter. But here we want to focus on one of the most important skills to our very Christianity—how to confidently listen to God from within.

ELIMINATE THE MIDDLE MAN

We all love to obtain direction from various earthly and outside resources. Many of us like to "hear God" through things like floods, rain, and earthquakes. We like to watch the nightly news and see if what is reported carries what might sound like a divine message. Sure, sometimes there is one, but just because that is the way we prefer to hear things doesn't mean there is always a message in these outside things.

Yet, for numerous reasons, we feel better if we can hear a "God-inspired message" from some outside source. We would rather hear "God" through a best friend than hear Him on our own. We feel we need to hear God from a prophetic word in a church service or through some unusual act of nature.

That isn't to say God will never speak through these things. Many biblical accounts describe how God used these outside things to speak to His people. Yet, we have to ask ourselves a profound question: Does the God who desires an intimate personal relationship with us only want to speak through a "middle man"? Does He always have to talk to us through the avenues of friends, family, circumstances, political events, or freakish acts of nature?

A true friend wants to talk intimately, face to face without the constant influence of the outside. Yet, for some reason many are afraid to hear from God this way. Of course some people are overly excessive about hearing God for themselves, and they run about telling everyone about their newest life-changing "revelation" that they feel came from God. Their desire to hear God for themselves is correct. Where their error comes in is that they forget to apply some important checks and balances, which we will cover later.

However, most people are on the other end of the spectrum. They can't ever feel confident that God speaks to them privately at all. They feel that the voice of their spirit is somehow "just them," so they discount the primary way in which God speaks. Therefore, a large number of Christians live feeling dependent on outside voices and resources to reveal God's direction for their lives. Yes, God uses these things, but He first wants us to live with confidence that we can hear Him in the privacy of our own hearts when He speaks to no one else but us personally.

No romantic relationship would feel right if either the man or woman was only expressing feelings through someone else. Wives, imagine if your husband could only send his "I love you" notes through a courier! Husbands, think of how you would feel if your wife had to have a spokesperson tell you how she felt. It would be completely odd!

Yet, that is so often how we want God to talk to us, via someone or something else. We want God to speak through earthquakes, rain, or storms. We would rather hear Him speak through the news reporter. What we forget is that God wants to talk to us directly without the middle man. One on one, person to person—that is the true picture of intimacy.

One of the most profound biblical examples of this is the prophet Elijah. He had to eliminate the "middle man" in order to have confidence with God. Outside things often did play an influence, but in order to accurately interpret the outside things, Elijah needed the skill to hear God privately with or without these other things. This way he wouldn't become confused about which things were actually a message from God and which things would lead to distraction or even outright deception.

THE MIDDLE MAN ADDICTION

It may be easier to understand why we are so reliant on outside voices and resources as the means to hear God's voice if we first understand what causes this tendency. Amazingly, the Bible carries incredible insight into the intricacies of our human psyche. God knows how we function!

We find some incredible examples in the story of Elijah in First Kings 19, when he was running in fear from the death threats of Jezebel. Of course, we know he was allowing fear to influence him, but give this mighty prophet some credit. Jezebel carried incredible political power, and she was very anti-God. She despised how Elijah carried the anointing of the Lord into her territory. She wanted to remove his influence and would willingly use all her powerful influence to do so.

So the Bible says that Elijah withdrew himself a full day's journey into the wilderness to hide from her (see 1 Kings 19:3-4). We can see several prophetic symbolisms in some of the things Elijah did after his flight from Jezebel. They reveal some of the things we tend to do that put us at risk for depending on a "middle man" or outside voices over depending on the voice of the Spirit within.

And when he saw that, he arose, and went for his life, and came to Beersheba, which belongeth to Judah, and left his servant there. But he himself went a day's journey into the wilderness, and came and sat down under a juniper tree: and he requested for himself that he might die; and said, It is enough; now, O Lord, take away my life; for I am not better than my fathers (1 Kings 19:3-4).

1.   He went to Beersheba: Relying on Past Events

The place Elijah immediately fled to in order to find God was Beersheba. Now there was probably nothing wrong with going to Beersheba by itself, and its history was rich with the miraculous things of God. We can undoubtedly assume this was why Elijah fled there. Countless Bible individuals had encounters with God at Beersheba, and it's obvious Elijah needed one!

Hagar had a divine experience with God in Beersheba, in which God appeared and spoke to her about the destiny of her son (see Gen. 21:14-20). It was also the place where Abraham made an oath of peace with King Abimelech (see Gen. 21:22-32). Abraham also called on the name of God in Beersheba (see. Gen. 21:33). Shortly thereafter, Isaac also had a divine encounter with God in Beersheba and made a similar oath with King Abimelech there (see Gen. 26:23-33). The name Beersheba means seven oaths because Abraham offered seven lambs to make a promise. Later, God divinely appeared in a vision to Jacob in Beersheba (see Gen. 46:1-5) and reiterated the covenant of blessing that He promised Abraham.

However, some historical accounts suggest that Beersheba eventually became a shrine. It was obviously known as a place where divine encounters occurred; otherwise Elijah probably wouldn't have been so quick to flee for refuge there. We find some biblical indication of Beersheba becoming a shrine in Amos 8:14, which says:

> *And those who swear by the shameful idols of Samaria—who take oaths in the name of the god of Dan and make vows in the name of the god of Beersheba—they will all fall down, never to rise again* (NLT).

Beersheba was originally a place dedicated to God, but we see here that people later began to worship false gods there (also see 2 Kings 23:8).

Then in Amos 5:5-6, we also find Amos the prophet warning Israel not to seek such places of divine encounter any longer. Bethel, Gilgal, and Beersheba are all mentioned, and we know these places to be Old Testament places of divine encounter (see Gen. 12:8; 28:10-22; Josh. 5:9, Judg. 2:1). However, the prophet warns the people to stop seeking these places but rather to again start seeking the Lord so they could live. It's obvious that Israel had become reliant more on a location and place of divine encounter rather than God Himself. Rather than trust in the Lord, they had placed their trust and worship in a location and past experience.

Shrines tend to speak of past miracles that have become a relic that people revert back to in a time of trial. We tend to do this in our modern-day Christianity as well. We repeatedly refer back to former revivals, such as the great healing revivals. We talk frequently about past experiences and miracles. We often feel more spiritual during worship when singing a certain song we used to sing at youth camp or at a ministry conference.

Actually, this is how denominations and camps are typically formed. They begin as a divine encounter with God but later turn into an idol of sorts. We start to worship the camp or experience over God without even realizing we are doing it. We are so busy talking about these past events that we miss God's voice inside.

Although there is nothing wrong with reminiscing about a past event or experience with God, we can't become reliant on these things to the point that we identify ourselves by them. Some people become quite adamant that they are of the camp of brother or sister so-and-so, or all they can do is talk about the revivals that happened in such-and-such city. They build their whole lives and ministries on these things and can't hear from God without being branded by the past. These people become dependent on everything familiar.

It seems quite certain that Elijah was falling into this human tendency. He wanted to go to Beersheba because, after all, that is where everybody else met God, so why not him? It was familiar. Of course, Elijah did have a divine encounter with God there, but notably that was the last time the Bible records such an event at Beersheba. Apparently, as soon as God saw that even this mighty prophet was falling into the tendency of relying on familiar, past events, He decided that was going to be the last supernatural occurrence there. From this we find that God taught Elijah the lesson of a lifetime, which we will cover momentarily.

Although we love those life-changing past experiences with God, and we can definitely learn a lot from them, we can't keep referencing them hoping we will be able to relive or resurrect them somehow. We need to let God lead us into new things because no matter where we are today, He has something fresh for us to walk in.

Relying on past events will keep you from hearing God for today. You run the risk of thinking that because God spoke to you in a vision three years ago, this is how He is going to reveal His will to you now, so you spend all your time focusing on the subject of visions. Constantly referring to the past to help you see your future causes you to stop looking inside and relying on the Holy Spirit within, and it heightens your need for a middle man in order to hear God.

2. He sat under a juniper tree: Attaching to the Situation

Once Elijah got to Beersheba, the Bible says he sat under a juniper tree (see 1 Kings 19:4). Juniper means "broom plant," from the root meaning "to yoke up or bind."[1] This root word indicates being bound or forcefully attached. Prophetically, this juniper tree represented the fact the Elijah had become so attached and consumed by the situation surrounding Jezebel that it was paralyzing him. It had consumed him.

We are all very familiar with this tendency! Most all of us can say that we have become so encumbered by something, at one point or another, that we just caved in under it. It was all we could think about, dream about, and talk about. The problem interfered with everything. This tendency has its roots in the spirit of fear, which causes other manifestations such as worry, anxiety, paranoia, shyness, stress disorders, and panic attacks, and it promotes numerous other physical illnesses.

People in this category are so busy rehearsing solutions and trying in their own natural abilities to fix their problems that they aren't listening to God at all. They are basing their levels of success and failure on what their situations are telling them. They look so hard at what is in front of them until that is the only voice they hear.

It is obvious that this is what Elijah was doing because he began to complain to God. He was so overwhelmed by his situation that he wanted to die. Elijah even slept under his juniper tree (see 1 Kings 19:5). Because the Bible made a point to mention that the tree was a juniper, I believe the prophetic indicator here is that Elijah was seriously bound to his circumstances.

We see this is true because in First Kings 19:10, Elijah begins to relate what he believes to be the truth through the eyes of his own trial.

> *He replied, "I have been very zealous for the Lord God Almighty. The Israelites have rejected Your covenant, torn down Your altars, and put Your prophets to death with the sword. I am the only one left, and now they are trying to kill me too"* (NIV).

He repeats his same complaint again in verse 14.

Notice how God responds. He allows Elijah to experience the big, dramatic encounter of Beersheba that he wanted. It's the same encounter we often want. Like Elijah, we are looking for that big, supernatural experience that will help us feel like we have overcome the terrible things we are dealing with right now. We start to want the experience itself more than we want God. I am convinced this was exactly what Elijah wanted—all because he was too focused on the supernatural past events of Beersheba, as well as his present problems.

Responding to Elijah's desire to experience God in a big way, God brought Elijah his desired earthquake, fire, and wind. However, the Lord made sure His voice was in none of them. They were nothing more than empty, natural circumstances from which Elijah was hoping to hear God's voice.

Most of us remember how the story ends. First Kings 19:12 says, *"And after the earthquake a fire; but the Lord was not in the fire: and after the fire a still small voice."* God wanted to talk to Elijah directly and didn't want to be confined to talking through all the surrounding, spectacular things.

Once Elijah was able to hear God through a simple voice, he was able to gain a right perspective on his situation, and he was able to find God's next step for his life. He learned that he wasn't all alone, as he once thought, and that there were 7000 others who hadn't bowed their knees to worship Baal (see 1 Kings 19:18). He had to face God on why he fled to Beersheba in the first place (see 1 Kings 19:13). He also received divine direction regarding God's will to anoint Jehu as the next king of Israel (see 1 Kings 19:16). Once he heard the simple voice of God, he left Beersheba knowing exactly where to go and what to do. It is also apparent that his fear of Jezebel melted away too.

Many people depend on hearing from God through outside resources rather than listening in their spirits simply because they do the two things Elijah did. They rely on past events and experiences, and they become too immersed in their present circumstances. Both of these things will deafen your spiritual ears to God's inward voice if you are not careful.

HIS VOICE IS IN YOU

We who are born again in Christ have been given an advantage that the Old Testament prophets didn't have. Though Elijah had to learn the principle of hearing God's simple voice without depending on the more obvious outside voices, he still didn't have the voice of the Spirit coming from within him. He tuned into the voice of God around him but not from within.

We have the Holy Spirit within us, and we can listen to Him from the inside. That is why in the New Testament we don't see God speaking commonly through things like a burning bush. Instead, we find God speaking through the indwelling Holy Spirit, as seen in Acts 16:6-7, when the Spirit forbid Paul's team from preaching in Asia. Of course, people still had outward experiences, such as visions (see Acts 16:9), but predominantly the believers listened to God and followed His will via the fullness of the Spirit within.

So for many the question is: How do you listen to the Holy Spirit within you? Here are some pointers that will help you accurately listen to God from within your own spirit.

SPEND TIME WITH GOD

This one is pretty simple: you can't expect to know the voice of anyone you don't spend time with. It will be much harder to hear the voice of the Lord when you don't regularly do the basic spiritual things like pray, read your Bible, and go to church. What you feed on and spend time doing is what will dominate your life. Even too much time doing the good and necessary things of life like work, chores, recreation, family time, and the like can be a distraction, and these things won't teach you how to hear the Holy Spirit.

The reason I recognize the voices of my husband and my children when they call me on the phone is because I spend time with them every day. The voice of a person whom you don't spend much time around will be unfamiliar to you. You need to spend time with God in order to recognize His voice.

In addition to prayer and Bible study, pray often in tongues. The reason this is also called "praying in the spirit" (see 1 Cor. 14:15) is because it connects you to the spiritual realm where the Holy Spirit is.

My husband and I do an exercise to help people realize how much praying in tongues comes from their spirits and not from their heads. We ask them to pray in tongues inside themselves silently, without opening their mouths, moving their tongues, or making any vocal sounds. Though praying in tongues silently inside themselves, we ask them to press in as hard as they can while making no sound. Then we ask them, after they stop, to indicate where they feel the pull coming from. In our experience, people will point to their stomachs or their spirits. They never point to their heads.

We have found just the opposite when people do the same exercise in their natural language, such as English. We have them shout a cheering phrase for their favorite sports team, like "Go Team!" as loud as they can. This time they don't feel the pull from their spirits but from their heads.

The pull you feel from your spirit is how you learn to hear from God. Spend time praying in the spirit often, and as you pray aloud or silently, tune in mentally to the sounds and sylla-bles of your spiritual language. Although you don't have to turn off your thoughts while you pray in tongues for your tongues to be effective, it is helpful to discipline your thinking when learning to listen to God. It will teach you how to listen to the Holy Spirit.

Of course, God will not always speak something then and there, but you should be open to it. Sometimes just the practice of focusing in on the pull of your spirit will help you recognize that pull when it hits you even while you aren't praying. Then you will start to recognize when it's the Holy Ghost. Some-times after praying in tongues for a while, start praying in your natural language and see what just "comes out" in your prayers. You may very well find revelation coming from your spirit! Remember, expertise comes with practice!

PAY ATTENTION TO FIRST IMPRESSIONS

When you are faced with a situation, particularly if you have been diligent to do the things needed to spend time with

God, listen to the first thing you hear. This doesn't mean that your first impression is always the voice of God, but if your habit is to spend time with Him, you will begin to recognize Him, and often the Holy Spirit will be the first voice you hear. Often when God speaks via a first impression, it comes fast and strong. Some people describe it as a decisive phrase, a short verse, or a sentence ending with an exclamation point!

For example, maybe you just got a pink slip at work saying you will be laid off. Then suddenly a jolting thought hits you that says, "Another job is already here!" or "They will hire you back very soon!" Write down those first and sudden impressions. This doesn't mean you should act rashly on these impressions, but note them and wait for the Holy Spirit to add faith and other confirmations to them.

In addition, when God speaks from your spirit, it often moves you differently than just a thought from your head does. Many times when God speaks from within you, it sounds like your own voice. That is because God speaks through you. Although it may sound a little bit like you, I have found that God's voice usually can be differentiated by the fact that it moves you and is stronger and more direct.

For example, referring back to our friends who prayed about moving to our city, the wife said she attended a class at our church during a brief visit in town. During the class she said she heard the words, "This is where I want you to be!" She said the voice wasn't audible, but it might as well have been because it made her entire insides shake. It was one of those times when she knew she wasn't making up the thoughts. She was moved so powerfully that after the class she immediately went and called her husband back home and said, "We're moving to Nebraska!" Within six months, they were here!

LISTEN TO THE "KNOWING" THAT STAYS WITH YOU

Sometimes God speaks to your spirit through a feeling about something that you cannot get away from. For example, again referring to our friends who prayed about moving to our city, the husband said he heard from God through just knowing it was so. He said, "I didn't hear any audible voice, but it was a knowing that came over a long period of time." He described it as something he just knew and it never left him.

With ample practice, every Christian possesses the ability to hear from God in his or her spirit accurately. There are, of course, confirming safeguards to this that we will build upon throughout the book. However, hearing God's will accurately for your life begins with listening to Him directly, inside of yourself, without the tendency to first depend on other things. God wants to communicate with you intimately this way so you can hear him confidently from within you!

ENDNOTE

1. *Strong's Concordance*, Hebrew #7574 from root #7573. Accessed via QuickVerse version 2008.

Chapter Three

USING SCRIPTURE TO FIND GOD'S WILL

Thy word is a lamp unto my feet, and a light unto my path (Psalm 119:105).

I s this scene familiar to you? You sit down with your Bible and cup of coffee and begin to thumb the pages. "Hmmm, Lord, what are You saying?" You look through countless verses, hoping to find one that jumps out to you. You need a verse that somehow speaks to the situation you are facing. Perhaps in a moment of desperation you even try allowing your Bible to fall open to a random page, hoping the first verse you see is the very thing you need to hear. Though many won't admit it, many have done it!

Then you find yourself glancing nervously at all sorts of verses. Some of them seem like the right verse, but then, when you're not quite sure, you thumb through for yet another, trying to miraculously come across the perfect one. Then it happens. You open to some verse relating to God's judgment or to a chapter listing genealogies! By now you're disillusioned.

Although it's certain that the Lord wants us to use His Word as a means for us to hear His will and direction for things, the process I've been describing couldn't possibly be the most reliable method for doing so. Yet many of us haven't found a more reliable way, so we stay with something similar to this. In this chapter, I will examine some principles that can help us be more accurate in how we go about using the Bible as a means to find divine direction.

LOCATE GOD'S SOVEREIGN WILL

God's sovereign will is His unchangeable plan and purpose. It is absolute because Jesus is the supreme ruler and we are submitted to Him. However, many Christians often refer to the phrase "the sovereign will of God" as something negative. They describe it as a trial or something tragic that happens that we may never understand, but because God is all wise, we just have to trust that God had a purpose in it.

Of course, we all know that God is much wiser and smarter than we can ever hope to be. So it isn't surprising that He will allow some things to happen that we don't fully understand. He won't be able to explain all the details to us simply because sometimes, in our limited understanding or present state of mind, we couldn't handle it.

I remember years ago when our oldest son Matt was barely in kindergarten and he asked me the meaning of death. I tried my best to explain it to him in kindergarten terms. He seemed to understand the meaning of death in the sense of the finality of it, but it upset him quite a bit. He kept asking more questions, and it was obvious he was fearful that this could or would happen to everyone he knew. I tried my best to explain to him that he shouldn't expect everyone he loves to die anytime soon, but nothing I could say would help him understand how it all works.

Finally, in desperation I had to say, "Honey, Mommy will have to help you understand it when you get older, because right now you just aren't ready." He accepted that as I encouraged him that sometimes we have a better ability to handle some things as we grow up.

We have to realize this with God as our Father too. Sometimes we just don't have the spiritual maturity or ability to comprehend certain things that He, the all-wise God, understands. However, we shouldn't automatically assume that just because something negative happened and we didn't understand the details, it was somehow God's sovereign will or intention.

Some people will argue that they believed it was God's sovereign will for a person they knew to have died of some illness. They will say things like, "Well, we prayed, but he still died. Therefore, God must have had a divine reason for it because our prayer for him to be healed was not answered."

There are hosts of reasons why certain negative things happen. Things like fear, distractions, mindsets, sin, lack of knowledge, religious demons, negative words, or just everyday bad choices can all play a part in attracting demons and hindering our prayers. The Bible warns how any of these things gone unchecked, either by us or others, can interfere with our blessings.

Nevertheless, especially when it comes to other people, we can't possibly know every detail surrounding a situation that may have played into the outcome. We may think we do, but we don't. With that in mind, we can't just automatically assume that because something negative happened, it was somehow God's sovereign will.

God's true sovereign will is really about something that many Christians overlook every day. It isn't as much about the negative things in life that we "don't understand." His sovereign will is more about His unchangeable promises. These promises are His sovereign will, and He wants us to understand them and learn how to receive them by faith. Of course, we may experience some successes and failures as we learn to walk in them, but regardless of our actions, His promises are nonetheless His unchanging, sovereign will. We find these sovereign, unchangeable promises in the Bible.

What is written in the Bible is God's sovereign will for you. You don't have to guess whether God wants it for you. You take these promises personally, as if God walked into your living room and told you this was His will for your life. God's will is found in His Word!

The Bible says in Psalm 138:2, *"...for Thou hast magnified Thy word above all Thy name."* What this means is that God has put His entire reputation on His solemn decree (see also the NIV). In other words, when God makes a promise, He is steadfast with it. His promises in the Scripture are steadfast, and He will not break them. God doesn't have some "divine" hidden will that is separate from His solemn decree written in the Bible.

There are countless Scriptures that promise us things like peace, healing, deliverance, and provision for our earthly needs.

When you are faced with a situation in life, first locate God's sovereign will found in His Word. Find a verse that has a promise for your area of need. Once you have established His promise, then you are locating God's sovereign will for your situation. Of course, challenging circumstances, fear, and even the devil will try to interrupt you from receiving it, but these things are much less likely to steal your victory when you are confident it is God's sovereign will.

For example, perhaps you are dealing with worry over your financial situation because you have lived much of your life financially challenged. Some could wrongly assume this was somehow God's intended plan for them and they have to accept their place in life. No! Instead, you must look for a verse that promises financial provision and see that as God's will for you, not your accustomed circumstance. This is called locating His sovereign will.

Rather than hope for some verse to randomly open to you, look specifically for verses that you know will solve your situation. Locate God's sovereign promises in the Bible on purpose. Read them, write them down, study them, and most of all—believe them!

Often, when we are in a trial or challenge or are dealing with something that is difficult to solve, we forget to do the basics.

Don't just rummage through your Bible at random. Get specific. Grab hold of the truths you know, and don't let go of them. Everything around you may be telling you that a breakthrough isn't meant to be, but if the Scripture promises it, then trust that it is God's sovereign will for your life. You may need to fight for it; the devil will use all kinds of things to try to steal it from you.

The problem is, we give up too easily sometimes. We allow circumstances to be more real to us than God's eternal promises written in the Scriptures. We allow the devil or even our own thoughts to talk us out of them. In some cases, the reason we don't find the promise we need in the Bible is because we just don't spend enough time in the Bible.

GOD'S WILL IN THREE VERSES

Quite a few years ago, I was preaching in another country at a conference. The meeting was not an evangelistic type of meeting that was directed to reach the lost. It was a church conference, sponsored by a Spirit-filled church. Most of the people in attendance were on-fire Christians and were heavily involved in church. There were also many pastors present.

As I began my message, I made a point about how important it is to rely on the truth of the Bible in the last days because of the evils that are increasing in the world. I encouraged the listeners that they needed to know what the Bible said at a moment's notice in the event they ever faced a trial. I remember posing this question and asking for a show of hands, "If you needed healing, how many of you, at a moment's notice, could quote at least three Scriptures that promise divine healing?"

There were a few thousand people in attendance, but when I asked that question, only a few people raised their hands—maybe 80 or so. Even many of the pastors couldn't raise their hands. Surprised that not more people knew at least three verses on healing, I decided to ask again. I thought perhaps my translator didn't hear me right so I wanted to be sure my question was correctly communicated. Yet, when I asked again, I got the same result. I went on to ask the same question regarding other Bible promises, such as financial provision, deliverance, and so on. Even fewer hands went up. I was stunned.

This was a group of people in a Spirit-filled meeting who dressed up, paid registration, and brought Bibles and notebooks to the conference. You could safely assume they were "churched."

I have done this test in other similar conferences and got a similar result, even here in the United States. At least people are honest. In order not to deliberately embarrass people, I don't typically ask the question directly now. Instead, I often relate the story, and it makes a great teaching point. I realize what a famine for God's Word is on the Body of Christ today. If we don't know the promises, we simply can't lay hold of them in a desperate time of need.

I would encourage you to memorize at least three verses on the major areas of need that most people deal with. These include divine healing, financial provision, deliverance and protection, overcoming fear, walking in peace, and overcoming sin and bad habits.

Now you may be one of those who can already recite three verses on all these subjects. Nevertheless, I would recommend you refresh yourself constantly. Don't always rely on memory; open again to the verses and reread them. Having been saved for many years, I realize that even when we know certain Scriptures, we can become lazy about doing them if we aren't diligent to read and meditate on them regularly.

People who are adamant about knowing the Bible and who spend time in it regularly are much more likely to be steadfast on God's sovereign, biblical promises when challenges arise.

TURN THE LIGHT ON

You have probably experienced just what I have: you were wondering what God's will and direction was about something, and then, during your routine Bible reading time, suddenly it was like the light came on. You weren't even looking for a specific verse at that moment; you just sat down to read. Yet somehow, you found yourself reenergized, and your situation didn't feel quite as unconquerable as before.

When you spend consistent time in the Bible, at times a random verse will jump out to you that speaks to your situation. You don't even have to let the pages "accidentally" fall open in hopes of it happening either!

I am reminded of a time when we were going through some challenges where the ministry was experiencing persecution. I was feeling the pressure of it one morning in particular. During my morning Bible reading that day I randomly opened to Luke 21:17-18, when Jesus talked about how God's people will be betrayed by close friends and hated for His name's sake. Suddenly, verse 18 jumped out to me. It says, *"But there shall not an hair of your head perish."* I immediately knew that was a word for us, and that God was assuring us that the ministry would not suffer any setback because of the present attacks.

This is why it is such a tragedy when we don't spend routine time in the Scripture.

Because the Word of God is anointed, it can make impossible situations seem conquerable, even when you aren't meditating specifically on a verse that applies to the thing you are facing. The Scriptures have the power of God on them, so they will produce faith in your area of need, even when you are reading something entirely different! Remember the famous verse in Hebrews 4:12:

> *For the word of God is living and active and sharper than any two-edged sword, and piercing as far as the division of soul and spirit, of both joints and marrow, and able to judge the thoughts and intentions of the heart* (NASB).

This verse means that every word in the Bible is God-breathed. They aren't like the words in any other book. These words are alive, and when read, recited, and meditated upon, they cause something to happen in your heart.

But notice that the verse says that God's words bring a division between the soul and the spirit. In other words, they will divide fleshly things from spiritual things. This is one of the main hurdles in finding divine direction—separating that which is from God from that which is coming from you or other earthly sources. The Scriptures will shed light on the things of God so they will stand out from the fleshly things and become the more obvious of the two.

For example, some Christians struggle to tell the difference between fear from the devil and a caution or warning from the Lord. They aren't sure if that gnawing feeling is God warning them or the devil trying to put fear in their hearts. That's what it means to divide between soul and spirit. The Word of God living in your heart will supernaturally make the division for you, and you won't live guessing about it.

Additionally, sometimes we struggle finding God's will about something because our own heart motives are tainted. Sometimes we don't realize it, or we just don't want to admit it. But this verse above also says that the Scriptures will begin to bring our heart motives to the forefront.

For example, perhaps you are trying to decide if you should buy a certain car. If you have spent time diligently in the Scriptures, you will find that God will put His thumb on your heart motive, even if you haven't read a single Scripture that points to your decision. If your heart motive is to buy a new car because your current one is getting older and your family truly needs one, then that will come out. If your heart motive is to buy a car out of covetousness because all your friends and colleagues bought new cars recently, then God's Word will reveal it to you.

If you heart is tender to the Lord, you will be willing to admit your own heart motives to yourself and repent when needed. Sometimes all God needs in order to give you divine direction is for you to check your heart and repent of a few things. An unchecked heart motive is spiritually blinding. Many people can't find God's will because they won't let the Word shed light on their own hearts. But if you openly make a habit of reading and meditating in your Bible, God will speak to you about areas of your heart motive that need adjusting.

You will be more successful at finding the will of God through the Scriptures simply because you habitually read and study them than because you frantically go looking for something in desperation. The Bible produces faith (see Rom. 10:17), even in times when you don't particularly think you need a jolt of faith. It produces caution for things, even when you didn't think there was something to be concerned about. These results are automatic because God's Word is living, and it imparts His sovereign will and decree for you both directly and indirectly.

Therefore, when you spend regular time in the Word of God, you can expect faith and revelation to be produced. Then when you are suddenly facing a situation in which you need direction from God, you step into it already at an advantage. You face it already prepared, with a sense of victory and confidence and a good initial handle on what to do.

That's why the Bible says in Psalm 119:105, *"Thy word is a lamp unto my feet, and a light unto my path."* It is a book of divine direction, and it will keep the light of God turned on inside your heart all the time. This makes it so much easier to find God's will and plan, even in the more difficult decisions of life.

GET IN THE PLAN

To help make things simple, perhaps you can remind yourself of a simple plan for using the Bible to find the will of God. Think of this acronym: P.L.A.N. It is *Prepare, Look, Ask,* and *Note.* Rather than keep looking for the pages to open to some random verses, try following this specific plan.

Prepare

Make a point to spend some Bible time every day, or at least most days. You will be surprised what just 15 extra minutes of undivided time in the Bible will do for you.

Look

When faced with a situation, look for a verse. It doesn't matter how familiar the verse is to you. If it applies, use it! Do a study and look for new verses about what you are dealing with as well. Dig revelation out of the Bible about your situation, or just dig out revelation in general!

Ask

Ask the Holy Spirit to reveal new things to you from the Word of God. Ask Him to show you places to look. Sometimes you may feel directed right when you ask Him, or the Lord may give something to you later when you least expect it. Listen to your pastor's preaching; he may read the very verse you need. If you ask the Lord to show you, He will bring it one way or another. Just ask and trust that God will show you.

Note

Note and write down the verses you hear and look up. You may find many verses, but I like to personally focus on two or three and just get them in my heart. Though I do review the others, sometimes if I try to keep too many before me every day, I don't stay focused. I often use little index cards to write down a couple key verses and carry them around in my Bible. I pull them out during my prayer times, read them aloud, and meditate on them. I also pray them out and thank God that they are working in my situation. I keep notes of the things I study and use them to build confidence that I am in the perfect will of God.

Also, take notes on the things God reveals in your heart as you go along. When you hear something, sense something, and so forth, write these things down as well.

There is nothing more rewarding than having confidence that you are receiving divine direction from the Bible. The more you use the Word of God this way, the more your skill and ability will grow. Sure, you will have some successes and failures, but rest assured that your successes will soon outweigh your failures as you grow in your ability to know God's will through the regular use of your Bible!

Chapter Four

HEARING GOD'S WILL THROUGH PROPHETS AND OTHER PEOPLE

For by wise counsel thou shalt make thy war: and in multitude of counsellors there is safety (**Proverbs 24:6**).

Everyone likes advice. Some people prefer it directly, while others like it indirectly. Those who like direct advice are quick to call a friend or call the prayer hotline. Those who don't really like people involved in their personal business prefer online advice or a self-help column that they can read privately. Still the truth is people are always hunting for advice about everything, including finances, occupational issues, homemaking tips, diet and exercise, and medical advice. Christians want to include spiritual advice as well.

In the human quest for good advice is the driving need for people to know their future destiny. In the non-Christian world, many seek out psychics, the horoscope, and similar mediums. Christians typically stay away from those things but tend to look to fellow Christians, church leaders, and also prophets. The truth of the matter is that people want to know about the unknown realm surrounding their lives and are hoping to get a glimpse into their future or their present situations so they can know how to respond.

There is no question that we all need good advice. The Bible says in Proverbs 24:6, *"For by wise counsel thou shalt make thy war: and in multitude of counsellors there is safety."* Essentially, what this means is that as we move forward in our endeavors of life, there is safety when we take in plenty of sound, godly advice. That is why the verse says we need a multitude of counselors. It takes more than one of them! We need several resources of people in our lives who can help us gain the right perspective with God.

In Chapter Two we talked about how to hear from God first before we take in the input of others. This is where most people make their mistakes. Instead of intently seeking God first, they immediately run to people. Seeking and hearing from God is a key skill that every believer must have.

However, once you have established that your pattern is to first get with God and listen to His voice, then you need to follow up with the right safeguards that other people provide. Others will help you determine if your hearing is accurate by providing balance. Because different people use different approaches, they can give you a bird's eye view into the situation that helps you see it from all angles.

Some Christians don't want anyone to cross-examine their revelations. I have met some believers who are "weirded-out" with strange things they claim God said to them. Then they think anyone who cross-examines their ideas is against them. Of course, no one loves constructive criticism, and not all input from others should have to come in that manner. We just need to be open and teachable to the input of others, knowing that we can all make mistakes, no matter how long we have served the Lord.

God places a great amount of confidence in people, and He uses people to help people. Once God has spoken to us privately, He will also follow up with input from people we can trust. We always need to be prepared for that. The struggle most of us have when it comes to the advice of people is that we fall into extremes. We either get so involved in the input of others that we forget to utilize our own ability to hear God, or we altogether ignore the importance of hearing from others simply because we don't want anyone else involved.

Nonetheless, as we learn to properly apply the input of others to receiving divine direction, there are key principles needed when listening to their advice. The main reason it is so important to have these principles is because of the human error factor. No matter who we get input from, all humans are subject to mistakes.

In this chapter, we will discuss how to listen to the much-needed safeguards of advice that come from the people around us without feeling apprehensive that we might be tripped up by their human shortcomings. We will also see that it is important not to either overemphasize or underemphasize the need for human input when seeking direction from God. We need a balanced approach.

GOD'S SERVANTS THE PROPHETS

There is a lot of emphasis on the ministry of prophets today as God has been restoring their importance in the Earth. We need prophets, but just like any other ministry, we still need to appropriate their function correctly. Some groups entirely discount the modern-day ministry of prophets, while others turn everything that moves into something prophetic. In those groups, practically everybody is a prophet.

Although we could spend considerable time validating the prophet's ministry here, we instead want to put this important ministry in perspective. We want to correctly appropriate the use of the prophetic in finding God's will for things. Anything, even if from God, used incorrectly can cause harm rather than the good God intended. Some have discounted prophecy and ignored it when it comes to them personally. Others have taken the use of prophecy to the extreme and made some costly mistakes.

The Bible says in Amos 3:7, *"Surely the Sovereign Lord does nothing without revealing His plan to His servants the prophets"* (NIV). We can see here that God makes sure that His prophets know the plans of God before He carries them out. However, in keeping with the context of the chapter this verse is written in, we can't take this to mean that God will always have a personal prophet available to us whenever we need divine direction. Obviously, that isn't realistic.

This chapter in Amos is speaking collectively about God's larger plans involving the nations of the Earth and God's people as a whole. It isn't saying that you must have a personal prophet speak to you specifically before you can be confident about God's will on something. God will sometimes use prophets in the church to speak personally to us. Yet, because one may not always be available, we can't depend on this as a predominant method for obtaining divine direction. Nonetheless, should the Holy Spirit provide the avenue of prophets, we need to know how to appropriate the prophetic words we receive.

Through our years of ministry, we have had numerous personal prophecies given to us. Some of them confirmed things we were already feeling, but others gave us insight into things we had no idea were on God's heart. They were totally new to us. Each type of prophecy requires a different approach, but some important principles should be followed for every type of prophetic word we receive.

In order to be brief, let's narrow our focus to four key principles for correctly handling prophecies. These principles can apply to how we approach both personal prophecy and corporate prophecy directed to a larger audience.

ALLOW THE PROPHECY TO MATURE THROUGH FAITH AND PRAYER

If you receive a prophecy, don't jump out and respond until you take it before the Lord and allow it to be bathed in prayer. Many prophecies, especially those that are bringing you "never heard before" information, need time for you to add faith to them.

Years ago, before we pastored our church, we were traveling full time in ministry. We received a prophecy during a service where the person giving it said, "The Lord says, you will pastor a church." Now at that time, pastoring a church was not in our hearts. In fact we thought, This guy is wrong. There is no way we will ever pastor! Well, surprise, surprise! Years later we pioneered, and now pastor, a very thriving church. However, in the interim, God needed a season of time to develop our faith and allow us to pray through it. We needed to mature so we could carry out the prophecy. At the time we received that prophecy, we weren't remotely ready to pastor!

It takes faith and strong prayer to bring certain prophecies to pass, especially those involving the pioneering of ministries or those pertaining to the higher levels of the miraculous. Even the mighty prophet Elijah who prophesied that it would not rain (see 1 Kings 17:1) had to pray his own prophecy into existence (see James 5:17).

Take notes on the prophetic words given to you and pray about them. Today you have the advantage of being able to get a recording of them. Transcribing your prophecies is a wonderful idea so you can keep them for close reference. Then pray about them and let the Holy Spirit develop them over time. If they are not of God, eventually they will become less pronounced and important in your focus. If they are truly from God, they will grow and develop. This is also true of prophecies given to entire groups of people, such as those for nations or churches.

WAIT FOR DIVINE TIMING

Some people make the mistake of running out and making rash decisions because of a prophecy. The best way to respond to prophecy is to wait patiently and allow God to establish the timing. Timing is key for success in following God's will through the use of prophecy. Sometimes it takes certain divine moments and events for God's will and purpose in the prophecy to be established.

You will recognize God's timing when He begins to open key doors for you and divinely provides the right opportunities. That is why you shouldn't jump into things just because you "got a word." Yes, sometimes God expects you to step out in the obedience of blind faith, but these types of prophecies will usually be spoken by those who know you and are familiar with your life, such as a trustworthy pastor.

Typically, when the prophets of the Bible gave divine instructions to someone, they had earned a trusted platform with their listeners. God is not going to demand that you do extreme things like quit your job, sell all your belongings, and move out of the country just because some prophet at a conference told you that you were called to help lost souls in foreign lands.

Give the Holy Spirit time to set things up for you. Sure, if you are certain the prophecy is God's will for you, there may be simple ways you can show God your faith and agreement, but in the larger decisions, let the divine timing play out. If you are submitted to God in your heart, He will surely help you get there. In fact, the Lord will set things up that will help you walk it out. You don't want to respond rashly out of ignorance and then get into something that wasn't the Lord or get ahead of Him in something you weren't ready for.

People make the same mistake with public prophecies given to a collective group. Many responded rashly to "prophecies" given years ago about the Y2K scare. People sold houses, built bomb shelters, and stocked up on emergency candles. In the end, none of these prophecies came to pass. I am sure many of the people who responded and spent their money wished they would have waited and made more prudent decisions.

WAIT FOR ADDITIONAL CONFIRMATION

If the prophecy you have received is from the Lord, expect the Holy Spirit to add to it. If you hear the prophecy and nothing ever seems to come along that feels like another piece to the puzzle, it's possible that the prophecy wasn't from the Lord.

At the time we received the prophecy that we would pastor a church, it felt like a mistake. Our focus at that time was traveling in ministry. Yet, some years later, things began to transpire, and the Holy Spirit began to put the desire to pastor in our hearts. By then, we had nearly forgotten the prophecy from years before, but we were reminded again when we suddenly began to sense we should start a church. After that, countless other confirmations began to come. We also began to receive additional prophecies regarding pastoring. Probably the largest confirmation was that our pastor felt God was leading us to go to Omaha and start a church. So even without additional prophecies, that confirmation was the one that sealed the deal.

Notice that we didn't just step out on prophecy alone; we waited for several confirmations because starting a church was a large decision. If God is going to use prophets and prophecy in order to reveal His will in our lives, He will bring situations and other things to come alongside to ensure us that the prophetic word is from Him.

RECEIVE PASTORAL GUIDANCE

There is a great deal of controversy over the importance of having our pastors weigh in on certain decisions in our lives. Again, we need a balanced approach. When it comes to obtaining pastoral input for things, we have to look at several factors. First, just as is the case with receiving input from prophets, direct and personal pastoral guidance may not be readily available for everyone. This is especially true of larger churches where it is virtually impossible for everyone to meet with the senior pastor or even an associate. However, we need to consider the biblical role of a pastor and realize that pastors *do* carry a God-given grace to speak into our lives. This can be directly or indirectly, depending on the how a particular church is structured.

Depending on your church's size and structure, you first need to see that even if you have little direct contact with your pastor or one of the associate pastors, the pastors still have a grace to help you nonetheless. Remember the Scripture in Hebrews 13:17 that says,

> *Obey them that have the rule over you, and submit yourselves: for they watch for your souls, as they that must give account, that they may do it with joy, and not with grief: for that is unprofitable for you.*

This Scripture appears to be pointing specifically to spiritual leaders, such as pastors, because the verse says that they watch and give an account for our souls. From this we can see a biblical, balanced message on having pastoral accountability in our lives.

Of course, in many modern churches this has become a touchy subject with all the concerns over pastoral control and church abuse. However, we still need pastors, and there is a valid biblical message about listening to their input and being obedient to their spiritual oversight.

This doesn't always mean you need to make a pastoral appointment or have direct pastoral input for making decisions. That isn't even possible in every church. In some smaller churches, the pastor is often more accessible this way, and people are able to ask him or her for godly wisdom and advice. In larger churches, it often falls to associate pastors or other leaders. In the end, even when endeavoring to seek pastoral wisdom, you still need the skill to hear God for yourself.

Over the years, when we have had appointments with those seeking our input on things, we like them to come prepared to share with us things they already feel God is telling them. That doesn't mean they should come already set on their decisions; otherwise there is no point in meeting with them. However, they should be able to tell us what they believe God is saying and then allow us to add to it and give them biblical and spiritual input on their conclusions.

Our expectation is that if people want to meet with us, they need to be open-minded to what we have to say and see if it lines up with the Bible and overall prudent counsel. Our prayerful hope is that our input will only encourage people in what they are already sensing that the Holy Spirit is saying to them. Sometimes it doesn't agree with them, but that is why we all sometimes need people to counter what we feel in our hearts. We can all make mistakes.

So with all the varying church structures, sizes, and cultures, what is the best line to follow when it comes to receiving the important biblical input of a pastor? There are a couple key guidelines that will help us incorporate this all-important ingredient for walking in the will of God.

HAVE YOUR PASTOR'S HEART

One of the best methods for obtaining pastoral input is to carry the heartbeat of your church and know how your pastors think, operate, and run things. Learn his or her anointing. You can't do this unless you are committed in your local church. If you only attend sporadically and you never get involved in serving in your church in some capacity, chances are it will be difficult for you to "feel" the spirit of it. You need to become part of the "woodwork" so to speak. When you do, you not only become part of the grace the pastor carries, but you also receive impartation from the anointing of the "house."

It's kind of like the "house" salad dressing in a restaurant. It has a flavor that no other restaurant has. It is unique for that establishment. Churches are the same way. Each carries a slightly different flavor and anointing. All pastors have a slightly different style of leadership and ministry. This doesn't make any particular one right or wrong, as long as the style is biblical; it just makes them different.

Again, a discussion of getting into the spirit of your church brings up the concern of so many who mention that their communities don't have a lot of choices on churches. They feel their church is acceptable but not what they would prefer. Regardless of what level you feel your church is on or what you wish it were, if it is your best option for a church, get connected anyhow. If you continue to feel that you should go there, then God can use it in your life nonetheless. You will be surprised at how the pastor will still carry a grace for you and be able to impart certain things into your life.

As you attend your church, absorb the preaching and apply it to your life. If you trust your pastor's godliness and doctrine, then you should work to apply what is preached. Of course, after having preached quite a few sermons, I know that pastors hit home runs in some messages while others are kind of dry! In the end, regardless of the pastor's delivery, you can still learn something from the sermon. Listen to the preaching, and you will be surprised how much guidance it will give you in your time of need.

As you gain the heartbeat of your church and pastoral leadership, you may also ask yourself the question, "What would my pastor do in this situation?" You may find yourself referencing in your mind one of his or her sermons or perhaps recalling a prophecy he gave during a service.

GET PASTORAL HELP ON BIG DECISIONS

When we felt the Lord telling us to start our church, we were blessed to have direct input from our pastor. I don't think we would have felt comfortable moving forward without it. However, I know not everyone has easy access to his or her pastor or pastoral staff for everything he or she deems important. I still think it is important to gain pastoral oversight on the larger decisions of life. These things would include getting married, stepping into full-time ministry, moving out of state or out of the country, or similar things that involve long-term or lifelong decisions. Some churches have guidance appointments available for such things. If yours does, I would encourage you to request one according to your church's guidelines.

We should all be able to make the less important decisions on our own with perhaps the input of just a spouse or close family member. However, it is a good idea to look beyond self and family when it comes to the larger long-term choices where we are trying to follow God. One common example is when pursuing full-time ministry.

When it comes to stepping into some form of full-time ministry that is not directly sponsored by your church, it really is a good idea to have a pastor give oversight and endorse the legitimacy of the plan. When possible, it is best for the local church to ordain and springboard most ministry endeavors. However, there is not always a clear-cut formula for these types of things because there are so many varying forms of church structure and ministry networks worldwide. Each of these has their own guidelines for those seeking full-time ministry.

I wouldn't even consider any full-time ministry endeavor without the direct oversight of a valid ministry that is personally familiar with my situation and ministry calling. In most cases, this would be a person's pastor. If my pastor didn't feel like my ministry efforts were from God, I can tell you that I would wait until things evolved and he felt confident to give me his endorsement.

I believe one of the reasons we have people in churches who are hurt and feel lost and abused is because of ministries that started themselves outside of God's will. Of course, not all "hurt" people in churches exist for that reason. Some are hurt because of their own carnality. However, many of these "churches" that began from e-mail ordinations and self-appointed endeavors have caused serious problems.

People connect themselves to these ministries and get confused and misled because they are subjected to half-baked leadership who have had little training, are very disorganized, and started without any form of valid or balanced oversight. Countless organizations are ordaining people whom they know little about. We need to submit ourselves to quality pastors who have valid fruit of ministry and allow our ministry callings to develop under these types of leaders.

If you are making a big decision, look for pastoral oversight from those ministry leaders who know you and aren't afraid to address any issues that they feel may hinder you in the years to come. Don't just reject the input of your local pastoral staff because you don't agree.

I have seen many people rise up without pastoral counsel and end up battle torn and wounded. When it comes to the big decisions of life, a prudent and well-experienced pastor has saved many people from a world of struggle, even when those people couldn't see the pastor's point at the time. For others, had they obeyed their pastor, they might have avoided some serious pitfalls in following God's will. I can testify that our pastor's input has helped save us from many detrimental mistakes.

THE ADVICE OF FRIENDS AND FAMILY

Our closest friends and family often know us best. They know our good qualities, and they also see us when we aren't putting on any frilly fronts! They get a front row seat into our shortcomings. They know who we are from all sides.

I often make the joke when preaching on family and marriage that when I was still single I thought I was the "perfect" Christian, but once I got married I began to think I needed deliverance from demons! I say that in humor only because when your spouse enters your life and thinks differently about some things than you do, suddenly your faults come into the light. You realize you aren't as perfect as you once thought!

Thank God for people who are close in our lives who can help us really see ourselves for who we are.

At the same time, it is also true that family and friendship relationships can get complicated. You have family, friends, and also, of course, those good ole friends of the family whom you have known for years. They each think their opinion is the most helpful piece of advice in your situation. Included with their advice comes their own ideals developed by their personal experiences, background, and preferences. Some of these pieces of advice are good input, while others can be carnal, worldly, or even just goofy!

Problems arise when you feel you have to let your friends or family members know that you just don't think their ideas are right for you. Suddenly you risk starting an uprising with other relatives and so forth. Before you know it, your brother calls to say that he feels you were a little too hard on mother and says, "You should have been more agreeable with her; after all, we need to be thinking of her health conditions!" Are you familiar with scenarios like this?

In addition, these conflicts can cause your own feelings to get hurt, and then your emotions start to work on you until the whole thing becomes confusing.

Examples, such as the one described here, make us realize that although we need family and friends involved in our decision making, we also need to know how and when to appropriate their input. Close relationships can be key to finding the will of God, but we need some important guidelines in order to know when to say yes or no.

Let's briefly discuss three key guidelines here. It is important to note that all of them really work together. What I mean by that is we can't really incorporate one without considering the others. We really need to keep all of them in mind when choosing to receive input from family and friends for knowing God's will in our lives.

YOU NEED HEALTHY RELATIONSHIPS

The reason many people get led off course through the advice of family and friends is because the relationships they are getting their input from aren't healthy ones. I am not a certified counselor, but my years of ministry and experience with people have helped me learn how broken people create broken relationships. This becomes very damaging to people's lives.

It's hard to trust input from people on which direction to navigate when their own ships have run ashore. It is further damaging when there is a great deal of hurt and negative feelings between people. Some family situations are difficult to repair unless those involved are willing to individually repair themselves.

Of course, that doesn't mean that if your family relationships aren't ideal that you can't ever receive from your relatives. What it means is that you have to keep the issue of their broken lives, in addition to your own areas of struggle, in perspective. Ask for the help of the Lord when it comes to handling relationships with family members. With God's help, attempt to steer yourself to the positive areas these people provide. When possible, allow yourself to receive from the healthier parts of the relationship, and try to avoid the negative ones.

If the broken relationship is a marriage, godly professional counsel or quality pastoral counseling may help. Just remember, the healthier any relationship is, the better your ability to give and receive valuable input between each other will be. That is because you both feel confident that the input is free of offenses, habitual sin issues, and wrong motives.

Unhealthy relationships also include those people whom you just know are not good for you. This may be a friend at school, a coworker, or a neighbor. Some relationships are strategically planted by the devil to get us on a wrong path.

This is how countless people get lured into adultery. They hang around someone they knew all along they shouldn't have.

They knew they shouldn't have been developing a friendship with someone of the opposite sex other than their spouse, but they did it anyhow. They chose to continue with this unhealthy relationship.

Many teens get into trouble because of friends who are leading them into compromise. Church people fall into carnality simply because they fellowship with other carnal Christians. This list goes on and on, but the truth is you must have healthy relationships if you want to receive godly counsel from the people in your life.

If you are looking to receive input for finding divine direction from people, steer toward the people with whom you have healthy relationships. Then follow up and be sure they are people who also know how to maintain healthy relationships in their own lives with others.

DIFFERENTIATE BETWEEN CLOSE FRIENDS AND CASUAL ACQUAINTANCES

Another reason people have a hard time getting the right input is because they look to people who aren't anything more than casual acquaintances. Someone may be your coworker or even a friend at church, but that doesn't mean he or she is qualified or prepared to speak into your life. This is particularly true when it comes to private issues that require someone who knows you better and has had the opportunity to gain a well-rounded view of the situation. You can't expect people who aren't very involved in your life to give you balanced input based solely on what you have told them.

When it comes to some of the bigger areas of life that we are seeking God's will for, we need to stay with the people close to us. Understandably, our close relationships may change and evolve over the years, but we need to seek the ones currently closest to us. These are the people who know our personalities and aren't afraid to tell us how some of our shortcomings might be playing into the present circumstances.

Often human nature likes to go to the people who aren't too close. Sometimes there is some value to getting an outside, unbiased opinion. However, this isn't healthy when the people you are seeking out don't know all the facts and you are only calling on them because you know they will tell you what you want to hear! This tendency gets a lot of people in trouble.

When possible, try to find people who know you well enough to be honest with you, even when the truth may hurt. For example, maybe you were hoping it was God's will for you to marry a certain person, and you wanted your friends and family to be on board with your decision. Instead, you need people who are willing to be honest and share their concerns, if there are any. This is especially true if you are making a major decision in life, such as whom to marry. A decision like this, if made wrongly without the input of those close to you, could damage your entire future.

SEPARATE THE SPIRITUAL FROM THE CARNAL

We all have had well-meaning people offer their counsel, but in the end, the only counsel worth heeding is godly counsel.

Jesus had to separate godly counsel from fleshly counsel with His own family. In Mark 3:20-21, we find that Jesus was in an intense and busy time of ministry. When His family and friends found out about how intense it was, they began to think He had lost His mind.

Probably out of nothing more than good intentions, they decided to try to stop Him. They probably thought Jesus was in over His head with all the crowds and demands. However, when His mother and brothers arrived where Jesus was, in verse 31-35, Jesus stood up and said, *"...who is My mother, or My brethren?"* (Mark 3:33). Then He followed up by saying, *"For whosoever shall do the will of God, the same is My brother, and My sister, and mother"* (Mark 3:35).

Jesus wasn't just trying to be deliberately rude to His family. He was separating their carnal behavior in this case from that which was spiritual.

Making this separation often seems one of the hardest tasks for good Christian people to do, especially when dealing with other Christians. They think that because some people in the church can talk a good talk, they are spiritual and godly. Yet, these good people sometimes forget to follow others' fruit. Jesus said we will know a good tree by the fruit that it bears (see Matt. 7:16-20). He didn't say we would know them by how well they can talk and convince us.

Romans 16:17-19 says:

> *I urge you, brothers, to watch out for those who cause divisions and put obstacles in your way that are contrary to the teaching you have learned. Keep*

away from them. For such people are not serving our Lord Christ, but their own appetites. By smooth talk and flattery they deceive the minds of naive people. Everyone has heard about your obedience, so I am full of joy over you; but I want you to be wise about what is good, and innocent about what is evil (NIV).

Here the Bible warns of those who can put on good speeches but have little to no godly fruit to back their words up. It tells us to keep away from them, not to go seeking for their input into our lives.

But the part I really want to highlight is found in verse 19. Notice how it says, *"Everyone has heard about your obedience."* In other words, Paul was telling his audience that ultimately the actions of people will become evident and be seen by everyone. This lets us know that at some point everyone will have visible fruit, good or bad, and we need to look for it before we trust them to give us counsel.

First, when getting counsel from people, we have to make sure it is godly counsel that lines up with Scripture. I am amazed at how many "Spirit-filled Christians" today don't hold themselves to the lifestyle the Bible teaches at all. They will get on the Internet and post comments emphasizing that they know what the Bible says, but their very actions reveal the opposite.

I can recall countless counseling sessions with people over the years where I would show people the Scripture again and again, but I could tell it wasn't being received. When this happens, more often than not people will leave my office and do exactly the opposite of biblical and godly counsel. The Body of Christ must get back to the Bible in this hour! We all need to hold ourselves accountable to it in our conduct, attitude, actions, and motives.

Make sure that whatever counsel someone gives you lines up with the Bible. If you spend regular time in your Bible, this will be much easier to do. If you don't, even the Bible that you *do* know won't come to mind as automatically, and you won't be as apt to obey it.

Second, make sure the people giving you advice have godly fruit. Something is wrong if they are sporadic about church or if, when they do attend, their body language reveals they aren't connected. Something is wrong when you see little signs of bad habits, like their spouse leaving for unexplained and extended periods of time. Look at their favorite hobbies and pastimes; sometimes issues are revealed through these things. If you happen to get a little closer to them and you begin to see issues with finances, like their credit card getting rejected at a restaurant a few times or their car being repossessed, then let it be a concern that maybe they have some character issues.

Usually, what we are able to see as church friends or acquaintances is only a small fraction of the mayhem that goes on in some people's lives behind closed doors. If you look hard enough, the kind of fruit people are growing on the trees of their lives will become visible at one point or another! The reason many Christians don't see it is they don't want to see it because of the compromise in their own hearts. They secretly want to hang around people with character issues and a little bit of compromise because it makes them feel better about their own secret vices.

If you stick to those who live godly lives and offer godly counsel, you will have a much better chance of staying on the right path.

God uses the counsel of people in our lives, and if our heart motives are in the right place, we are more likely to find those who will help steer us in the right direction. Be assured that God does bring the input of prophets, pastors, and even friends and family to help make us well-balanced people who don't have to feel all alone when it comes to making good decisions in life.

As you listen to God's will for you, regardless of how big or small your issue is, God will add people into the mix to act as a safeguard and to bring balance into the situation.

As you seek the Lord, write down the input of others in a journal. Keep the prophecies that come before you within easy access. Write down the advice of your pastors, family, and friends. As you collect the input of others, the things that are truly from God will begin to be repeated. You will likely start to see agreement and a consistent message begin to form among all the input you receive.

If you follow these few key principles, you will more readily be influenced by those who want the best for you as you follow the Lord.

Chapter Five

HEARING GOD'S WILL THROUGH CIRCUMSTANCES AND PERSONAL EXPERIENCES

...suddenly there shined round about him a light from heaven (Acts 9:3).

E veryone heard it, but they couldn't see anything. It was the sound of an awesome voice that called out his name. The light was so bright it threw him to the ground where he lay trembling and shaking. Everyone with him stood there void of words to describe what had just happened. The whole experience left one of them totally blind, but it wasn't the blindness that so intently affected him.

He was shaken to the core well before he stood up to discover he was completely blind. It happened when he heard the voice from Heaven say his name, *"...Saul, Saul, why persecutest thou Me?"* (Acts 9:4). Most of us know the story in Acts 9 of the incredible conversion of the apostle Paul, who was at one time one of the greatest enemies of the Church. Then one day his life was turned upside down by a supernatural event.

His conversion was nothing short of miraculous. Few can boast in saying that they became a born-again Christian because they saw a bright light that threw them to the earth, followed up by an audible voice from Heaven.

Yet, we need to determine if such experiences should be the expected norm when trying to find the will of God. We don't find Paul ever having an encounter quite like this again, in which he was given such specific directives regarding God's will that established the foundation for his entire future ministry. However, we do see accounts where Paul was led in God's will by the Spirit within (see Acts 16:6; 27:10).

At the same time, there are some occasions when God speaks through things like everyday circumstances or even unusual supernatural experiences like Paul had. We often have a hard time knowing which of these circumstances contain a message from God and which ones are nothing more than circumstances.

We have an even harder time differentiating which circumstances contain a divine message when it comes to catastrophic world events and supernatural experiences because we think that these big events must undoubtedly be from God. However, just because something is supernatural, catastrophic, or a personally impacting experience doesn't mean that a message from God was in it. Some of these things aren't from God but come straight from the devil!

When America was attacked on 9/11, I remember watching on television countless preachers, and even a few secular commentators, push the idea that the event was surely an act of God's judgment. People said the same about Hurricane Katrina and similar catastrophic events. They emphasized that God was sending America a message. A further indicator of this human tendency is the fact that many insurance policies refer to such types of events as "acts of God."

The trouble is no one ever puts any blame on the devil, who comes to steal, kill, and destroy (see John 10:10). We automatically and erroneously assume that everything bad that happens is God sending a message of correction or judgment.

This isn't to say that God can't send a message through some event such as I have mentioned, but we really don't see God using the elements to judge the world in the New Testament until the Book of Revelation, when the era of grace on Earth comes to a close. We see these events much more under the Old Testament before Christ entered the world.

Keeping within the lines of the New Testament era of grace, I am of the mind that we are still under the umbrella of what the angels announced at Jesus' birth. They said, *"Glory to God in the highest, and on earth peace, good will toward men"* (Luke 2:14). They were telling the Earth that God was extending the entire world a treaty of peace, that His hand of judgment was being stayed in order to allow all people an opportunity to receive His extension of grace and mercy.

Of course, we know that catastrophes are in fact happening worldwide. However, perhaps we need to consider that these aren't so much about God's judgment right now but are rather the Earth responding to the sin within it. We see this in Romans 8:22, which says, *"For we know that the whole creation groaneth and travaileth in pain together until now."* This means that the Earth is suffering in a worldwide, common struggle. No region of the planet is exempt from natural catastrophe.

The wickedness and continual sin in the Earth is repeatedly sowing itself into the soil, just as the sin of Adam caused the ground to be cursed in Genesis 3:17-19. The Earth is groaning under the weight of people's sins as they continually increase. Undoubtedly, certain nations that have advocated evil are reaping even higher catastrophic results from their sins, which are manifesting in the elements and the soil. I believe this is why we are seeing the elements convulsing in such turmoil, and both poverty and famine are rampant in many parts of the world. The Earth is reaping forth what people have sown into it (see Gal. 6:7).

Yet, we know from Scripture that the time will come when the Righteous Judge of the Earth will bring the final gavel down. When the growing hardness of people's hearts exceeds the Church's ability to spread this message of God's love and grace, the Lord will be left with no choice but to the judge the world (see Matt. 24:12). We see these catastrophic judgments listed in the Book of Revelation.

The Bible warns us that as we progress closer to that time, people's hearts will be "without natural affection" (see 2 Tim. 3:3). This means the mass population will gradually lose the natural milk of human kindness and will develop a hardness of heart. They will increasingly become hardened to the Gospel message of mercy. We are seeing this progression even now, but ultimately the time will come when God's true era of judgment will wipe the slate clean.

Does this mean that God will never use circumstances to speak a message? No, but we can't assume that these events are somehow automatically the voice of the Lord either to us or to the sinful world around us. Yes, they serve as warnings and yes, these events will cause some to reconsider their ways. But, unless in the midst of such an event people have a true encounter with God like Paul did on the Damascus road, their reconsideration is usually temporary.

The hearts and minds of most Americans are not more driven toward God today than they were before 9/11. If anything, they are more hardened, and the mass population has quickly forgotten what happened. I don't think 9/11 has given the secular world a life-changing hunger to seek the Lord.

Think about it. If an earthquake happens in some country, is it causing people to suddenly seek the Lord? Sure, the event itself may send a sobering message that shakes people—literally—and it may even help some become more open-minded to the Gospel.

However, in Luke 9 when the disciples wanted to call fire down on the enemies of Jesus, the Lord responded by saying, *"…Ye know not what manner of spirit ye are of. For the Son of man is not come to destroy men's lives, but to save them…"* (Luke 9:55-56). Romans 2:4 says that it is the goodness of God that leads people to repentance. Then verse 5 follows up by saying that those who refuse to repent are storing up for themselves judgment that will be carried out on Judgment Day. Perhaps we need to consider that God is reserving the catastrophic judgments for the day of His wrath.

In the meantime, based on these verses, I don't think we should assume that worldwide tragedy is God sending a message or even speaking through these particular circumstances.

So this brings us to the question about how we should determine which circumstances and events actually carry a divine message from God. Many people get hung up on circumstances and experiences and adapt their entire lives to them without first making sure they are legitimately from the Lord. There are key ingredients that should be present for those occasions when God uses circumstances to lead us into His will.

BIBLICAL EXPERIENCES

Being biblically based is a commonly mentioned principle, but it's probably the most important. Many Christians these days have become forgetful of what the Bible has to say on many issues. They are falling into all sorts of erroneous ideals because their knowledge base in the Word of God is so small. Some simply haven't developed the necessary Bible study skills in order to weigh the things they experience against the Scripture. They credit God with everything that happens, but they don't measure these events against God's character found in the Bible.

We have probably all heard the saying, "Experience is the best teacher." Yes, experience can teach us many valuable lessons. At the same time, there are countless experiences in life that don't come from the Lord, and the "lessons" we have learned from them was not from Him at all. In fact, it was the devil attempting to taint our thinking.

For example, if a kid is severely bullied at school, the whole experience causes emotional damage that needs undoing. If not dealt with, the victim runs the risk of having problems later that may keep him or her from responding correctly to God in certain areas. There is nothing positive and biblical to be learned from the experience. In fact, it is nothing more than an attack of the devil. In this case, experience isn't the best teacher. It rather serves as a hindrance and detriment to normal healthy emotions.

No doubt, God our Father can take even the circumstances that came from the devil and turn them into something good. The Bible says in Romans 8:28, *"And we know that all things work together for good to them that love God, to them who are the called according to His purpose."* God can take any situation the devil meant for evil in our lives and turn it around for good, and we can undoubtedly use it to help someone else. This doesn't mean, however, that God planned the whole experience to teach us something.

People think this way all the time when it comes to sickness and disease. They think the experience of a certain illness was designed by God to teach them something or to develop their character. That isn't to say that we can't learn some key lessons by the things we walk through, but we need to make sure the lesson learned aligns with what God teaches us in Scripture. Furthermore, God couldn't have purposed it if the experience wasn't in agreement with the way God dealt with our fellow Christians in the Bible. That would go against what God has revealed to us about His character.

Under the New Testament era of grace, we find no examples of God putting sickness and tragedy on His people in order to send them a message and ultimately make them better people for it. We saw this type of judgment in the Old Testament, when God's people, Israel, rebelled against the Lord, but they didn't have the blood of Jesus Christ advocating on their behalf.

Yet, even under the Old Testament pattern, God always gave them an extension of mercy and an opportunity to repent before His righteousness consumed them.

Jesus' blood now stands between us and the judgment of God. In fact, this is the message of God to the world right now. In the New Testament, we don't find God putting tragedy on people in order to reveal His will to them. Of course, the Bible gives plenty of other reasons why people can come under these types of attacks, and the law of the Earth is that we reap what we sow (see Gal. 6:7).

Nonetheless, we still can't assume God was behind a tragic event because we don't see God doing this type of thing to Christians in Scripture. We would be more biblical to see these things as the devil and, in some cases, the results reaped from our own wrongdoing.

We have no example in the New Testament of God using sickness as a method to develop our Christian character or give us some form of divine direction from it. In the case of the apostle Paul having become blind, it was undoubtedly because the light from Heaven was too bright for his eyes (see Acts 9:3-8). But notice that his condition was extremely temporary, and after it happened, the first place the Spirit directed him to go was the very place to receive his healing!

Again, God can take a negative situation and use it for our good, but that doesn't mean it was His will and plan for it to happen. If God is going to use a circumstance in our lives to reveal His will for us, it will come in the form of something that is biblical and that follows the types of things that we see happening to people in the Bible.

Similarly, if God is going to speak to us through a supernatural experience, it will follow the examples of the types of supernatural things we see happening in the ministry of Jesus and the early church. Some people in Christendom today describe unusual supernatural experiences that sound more occult-like than biblical. Whether it is a personal experience, tragedy, natural catastrophe, or some supernatural event, we must make sure we can find something that validates it in the Bible, particularly in the New Testament. God is the author of the supernatural, but we do need to keep our supernatural experiences within the boundaries of the New Testament pattern.

A GENUINE ENCOUNTER WITH GOD

We can see from Paul's experience that he had a total heart transformation. What he experienced was much more than a supernatural event; he had a personal encounter with Jesus Christ that changed him. It wasn't just something he wrote home about or had published in a local Christian column so he could boast, "Hey look what happened to me!" No, it changed him in a radical way and reestablished His entire future. The experience caused him to be forever dedicated to the Lord. A supernatural experience or catastrophic event that doesn't transform lives for God is probably nothing more than a circumstance.

Like me, I am sure you have met Christians who tell of great supernatural encounters and personal experiences, but they live very carnal and even sometimes backslidden lives. Some talk of daily life experiences that they believe are from the Lord, but they never seem to become better people because of them. Their character never seems to improve. They still divide churches, mistreat people, and do some sinful and deplorable things.

That isn't to say that people's experiences weren't from the Lord just because they later chose to sin. What it means is that when something occurs in your life that is from God, it should make you look inside yourself and examine who you are as a person to the point you are able to make some real changes.

Years ago, a lady visited our church for a short period of time who constantly talked about all her supernatural encounters and experiences. The problem was she was one of the most inconsiderate and undisciplined individuals I have met. She was entirely prided on these experiences, to the point that she was so ethereal she couldn't carry on a normal conversation with people. All she could talk about was her deep revelations and heavenly visions. Her version of Christianity came across very shallow and seemed to lack a genuine love for the Lord Himself. It seemed more as if she was just trying to get attention by talking about all these things.

In fact, she couldn't fit in with anyone. We eventually found out that she had been asked to leave her previous church, and to no one's surprise, she didn't last long at ours either. She didn't think anyone was on her level of revelation. My problem was that her vast number of spiritual experiences seemed to have had little effect on her ability to be useful in God's Kingdom, and they didn't improve her character.

When God is using an experience or circumstance to guide you, He will make it have enough of an impact that it will drive you to become a better, more mature person. You should come away knowing God more intimately. The experience or circumstance should also be able answer certain areas of need in your own life.

I am amazed at how many Christians talk about how they have these deep experiences with God, they but have no fruit to show for it. Their lives, families, and finances remain a mess year after year. If God is really speaking through the circumstances in your life, then the effect on your heart, mind, and walk with God should become evident.

A CLEAR AND DEFINITIVE MESSAGE

Have you ever had a dream and woke up and remembered some of the things in the dream and wondered if God was trying to tell you something? I think we all have. There are many helpful books written on how to correctly interpret dreams, so we won't cover all that here. What I do want you to know is that if God is saying something in a vision, dream, circumstance, or experience, the message should be clear. That doesn't mean you will always figure it out at the first moment, but the clarity will begin to develop in an obvious, progressive way.

I often hear people say things like, "Well, I know God must want me to learn something from this horrible mess I am in, but I just wish I knew what it is!"

Although God can't always reveal every detail of certain things until we are ready to handle them, He also isn't up in Heaven trying to keep you in the dark! Whenever God spoke to people in the Bible, His messages came across loud and clear. They didn't have to try and piece this and that together and somehow "make it fit."

As of late, I hear quite a few people and ministries piecing together bits and pieces of different circumstances or world events and then trying to make something prophetic from them. They say things like, "Because the storm happened on the seventh day, it must mean that God was perfecting something in that region because seven is God's perfect number!"

I am not discounting all prophetic symbolism in regard to events. It does have its place. However, I want to make sure that if we use prophetic symbolism, we balance it with the other key ingredients needed for locating God's will through circumstances. We need to ask if the event is biblical in nature and if the God of the Bible would use this type of event to speak. We need to determine if the message is clear and if it causes a heart change in its intended audience.

Half of the time, when people go crazy with prophetic symbolism, such as I have described here, they don't know exactly who the supposed audience is and have little biblical basis for what the specific message for the listeners is supposed to be. Numerous times in such cases, we see the people who were supposed to be the intended audience are continuing on with their lives as if God was nowhere around. To top it off, often those who say the event was a divine message aren't doing anything to bring the Gospel message to those affected.

When God sent the divine message that Nineveh was going to be overthrown, He first sent Jonah in order to make the message clear. He gave the people a clear extension of mercy with an opportunity to repent. The message was so clear it reached the city leadership. Often when people see natural disasters and earthquakes, they publish them as God sending a message, but they don't investigate how any specific message from God is made clear to the people affected.

When a great famine came on the land during the days of Claudius Caesar, God gave the people advance warning through the prophet Agabus (see Acts 11:28). The event didn't just happen while everyone sat around wondering what it might mean.

We see a lot of this today. Few in the Church can seem to foretell events. Instead, they just try to piece them together after they happen, attempting to locate some divine message in them. Even if the Spirit doesn't forewarn us of something, if the Lord has a message from it afterward, the message should be clear to the intended audience. When Paul had his experience on the road to Damascus, the message was so clear he couldn't mistake it!

Because constantly changing circumstances and events can be very misleading, I think we need a very careful standard for using them as a means for locating the will of God. In other words, if the message isn't clear or deeply impacting, like it was with Paul, then we need to use caution.

If you wake up from a dream having to guess if it was a spiritual dream, and no one else is sure what it means either, then I would reconsider it. Too much ice cream before bed might have been what brought on the dream!

MAKING CIRCUMSTANCES FIT YOUR WILL

Sometimes we get set on something we want so we try to find reasons why we think God wants it for us too. Now some things God does want for us because they are biblical promises. Things like health, peace, wisdom, and provision are all from God. However, sometimes we want God's will to conform to the things we want, and yes, perhaps the things we want are things God has promised. However, we get off base if we are attempting to obtain them through wrong methods.

For example, maybe you want a certain job, and you are wondering if it is God's will for you. Of course, God wants you to have a good job. You know that this particular job might keep you out of church more and even demand more time away from family. Yet, you reason to yourself that it pays more and will help you pay off some bills. In the end, you want to know God's opinion on it, but another side of you is set on that job!

Here is where I have seen many people make mistakes. They want something so badly they ignore key principles for locating the will of God and start looking to all kinds of strange or coincidental circumstances in order to find it.

Returning to the example, as you think about that dream job, you suddenly notice a magazine at the dentist's office with a famous person on the front cover who is talking about the very career you are considering. "That must be God!" you say. Then, if you're not careful, you begin to look to almost any situation and try to turn it into a "God thing."

When you are already determined about something, you should be extremely careful about looking for circumstances that "confirm" your predetermined desires. This scenario makes it easy to forget other important and more reliable principles for locating God's will. The tendency is to start using circumstances and events as the predominant source for finding divine direction.

When that happens, people tend to start believing goofy things like angels appearing in cookies, "confirming" license plate numbers, or superstitious objects, times, and dates. They want some strange circumstance to confirm what they already believe, so they begin to turn almost anything that happens into some kind of divine encounter. The whole thing really does get into superstition, and people start missing God. They often quit listening to the key safeguards coming from the trusted people in their lives as well.

Though God may want to reveal a piece of His will for you in some form of event or circumstance, you must purpose to not go looking for it. Let those things present themselves to you the way they did for Paul, and make sure they line up with the right principles for hearing God. If it's truly from the Lord, like Paul's experience was, you will know! Consider that what Paul received on the road that day was definitely not within his predetermined future plans!

In the end, I believe God uses circumstances and natural events to reveal things to us, but I don't think they should be our predominant source over other key principles, and they should be balanced against other methods. When we do think God is saying something through experiences or circumstances, if we keep these key principles in mind, we won't miss God's plan.

Chapter Six

TOO MANY VOICES; WHICH WAY DO I GO?

...and His voice thundered like mighty ocean waves
(Revelation 1:15 NLT).

L ooking at all the different methods God uses to speak His will into our lives, we could get overwhelmed. Sometimes we look at all the choices and voices of input before us, and we wonder which fork in the road is the right direction. With listening to our own spirits, taking in the input of other people, and studying what we find in the Bible, at times it feels like a lot to absorb.

After countless years in ministry, I realize every day holds a new set of decisions, and much of any given day is spent making these decisions. Not only do we have to locate God's will for one area of life and ministry, but on any given day we also have to make decisions about a long list of other things as well. How do we pull it all together and make sense of it all?

Thank God we have the Holy Spirit who guides and leads us into His will, often when we don't even realize we are being led! In Chapter One we talked about how we can rest assured that even when we don't feel like we know which way to go, God will ensure we won't miss it. He has an incredible way of taking the choices we make in ignorance and turning them around so we end up right where we need to be.

Yet, when the choices coming our way seem endless, we have to be able to narrow down a direction so we can carry out everyday life. We want to feel confident that we are making good decisions about the daily things surrounding our lives. No one wants to feel like they are waltzing through life in some kind of guessing game. Instead, God wants us to be at peace and to feel confident that we can make daily decisions in a resolute way.

KEEPING YOUR WILL IN CHECK

One of the biggest culprits for why we don't feel we can make precise decisions in line with God is that our heart motives get off. We let our own wants and needs come before what God wants and really what is best for us in the long run. When this happens, we start to listen to all sorts of influences.

You know how it goes—it's that new television or car that you want. You know it wouldn't be a wise decision to charge it, and you even feel the Holy Spirit caution you, but in the end, your want wins out! Too many people make these choices and then are later sorry.

This is often why we aren't confident about our abilities to follow the will of God. We let too much of our own will and desires get in the way. This ultimately causes us to lose confidence and creates confusion. It also opens the door to the influence of the devil. The most precise way to follow God's will accurately is to make a daily decision to submit our will to Him.

This is easier said than done, and it requires a daily commitment. We need to make a conscious decision every day that the Lord gets the final say when it comes to our plans and pursuits in life. The Lord should be in charge of where we work, where we live, whom we marry, and where we attend church. However, sometimes, because of our own flesh, we rise up and make our own choices and then pretend God was the one who told us to do what we did.

Countless believers do this. It is amazing what some will justify and twist in order to make their actions sound like God was in them. I have seen people do this when it comes to the person they are to marry. They will date and marry somebody who isn't sold out to the Lord or who has some cautionary behaviors, and they try to make everyone around them believe God is behind the marriage. As pastors, we have counseled numerous people along these lines. Some we told that we didn't feel good about their marriage plans, but they went forward anyhow. Many of these marriages have ended up in a mess, some in divorce.

Many people backslide and quit attending church because they have made a habit of listening to their own will and desires. Some Christians get caught up in hanging around other carnal and divisive Christians because their own will is at the forefront and it makes their fleshly habits feel justified in some way. They get offended at the church for various reasons, but they refuse to work through it and find healing. Some will leave a good church because they don't want to deal with certain issues in their life, and then they act as though God spoke to them that is was "time to move on." But often the real reason they go the way of hurt and offense is because their predetermined will is hardening them from doing what God expects. Eventually, they begin to believe that certain behaviors and mindsets, even those that go against the Bible, are somehow in line with God's will.

The longer you habitually convince yourself that your will is somehow God's will, the less you will be confidently able to locate His voice in the midst of all the various things trying to influence you. Your ability to follow God's will in your life begins with submitting everything to Him. This might mean that you have to give up certain friends. It may mean that your attitude will have to get adjusted. Your schedule may have to change. Following the will of God may sometimes demand that you make choices you don't always want to make. There will be things you will have to perhaps give up or add to your life.

The fact that we are Christians means we are to be like Christ. We simply cannot live life unto ourselves and expect to feel confident that we are following the Lord like we should. For some Christians, this problem has almost become an epidemic.

Every one of us who wants to be confident about making precise decisions according to the will of God needs to go back to James 4:15, which says, *"For that ye ought to say, If the Lord will, we shall live, and do this, or that."* Verse 17 just below it also says, *"Therefore to him that knoweth to do good, and doeth not, to him it is sin."*

If you want to narrow the countless voices and options before you, one of the most significant choices you can make is to simply decide your life is not your own. This means that sometimes God will ask you to do things you simply don't want to do or that you don't deem important. He will ask you to love people who aren't easy to love. He will ask you to be careful about the things you say. It also means you may have to let go of some often-excused, but bad habits, such as controlling or manipulating others, laziness, or bad financial practices.

The best Bible passage that expresses what I want to communicate is Psalm 15:

> Lord, who may dwell in Your sanctuary? Who may live on Your holy hill? He whose walk is blameless and who does what is righteous, who speaks the truth from his heart and has no slander on his tongue, who does his neighbor no wrong and casts no slur on his fellowman, who despises a vile man but honors those who fear the Lord, who keeps his oath even when it hurts, who lends his money without usury and does not accept a bribe against the innocent. He who does these things will never be shaken (NIV).

We learn here that the ones who will never be shaken in life and will remain safely in God's presence are those who do the things this Psalm describes. It's true that some Christians are getting shaken in life and are struggling to locate God simply because they don't submit their will to the things God expects in this Psalm.

If we want to be in God's will, we can't enforce our will through secret sin. We can't lie and gossip against others or befriend carnal people. We must also keep our commitments and promises and use our money for good purposes. God's expectations regarding these areas are found in this Psalm, and if we do them, we can be confident that we will hear God's voice over the countless influences out there.

Proverbs 16:3 says, *"Commit thy works unto the Lord, and thy thoughts shall be established."* The NIV says, *"Commit to the Lord whatever you do, and your plans will succeed."* If we do things God's way over our own, the automatic result is that God will keep us safely in His will.

KEEP A JOURNAL

One of the best things any of us can do for ourselves is to write important things down. As we are praying through certain things, we should track our progress and answers to prayer. Most of us would be amazed at how accurately we hear from God if we could go back and review some of our decisions.

Perhaps you are praying about taking that certain job or having a particular medical procedure. As you listen to God in your heart, look to the Scripture, and take in advice from family and friends or even prophecies you have received, it helps to put them all on paper. Writing things down narrows the playing field, and you will likely begin to locate one consistent message among them. You may notice that a prophecy came along that lined up with the thing you have been feeling in your heart.

A journal may make it much easier to weigh out the good from the bad. Then when your somewhat controlling relatives give you advice, you will be able to see where their input isn't lining up with all the other things. A journal may very well help you weed out the voices that aren't from the Lord.

You probably know that writing down the things you sense and feel in prayer is key as well. As you pray in the spirit, jot down the things that come to you and include them in your journal. The idea is to see a consistent message develop. Journaling what comes to you also helps you hold yourself accountable so that you don't forge forward on your own "word" alone.

When you write these things down and your friends and family or even your pastor disagree with the thing you may be thinking is God, then perhaps it means you should use caution. If you have prophecies that seem to warn you from getting involved in something, then the Lord may be trying to keep you from making a mistake. A collective list is a great tool in helping you define which voices, input, and pieces of advice are from the Lord.

THE SOUND OF HIS VOICE

Years ago when we were first starting in the ministry, we had numerous challenges. We were trying to find direction on how the Lord wanted us to pursue ministry, we were trying to make ends meet financially, and the list goes on. There were so many things to sort out that we felt like we were getting lost in the shuffle. Have you ever been there?

During that time when were trying to hear some direction from God, the Lord spoke a very encouraging word to my husband that I never forgot. God said, "Hank, My ability to speak to you is greater than your inability to hear." From that time on, we began to settle down and trust that God's voice was going to come through loud and clear whenever we needed it.

Though the voice of God can come in the form of a whisper deep within you, it will have a sense of loudness about it. In other words, His voice is forceful in such a way that it alerts you. Like I said in Chapter Two, the voice of the Lord in your spirit often sounds like you, but it comes with greater strength. After hearing it, you have this strong feeling or confidence that it was the Lord talking.

We need to remember that the Bible describes the voice of the Lord as being very loud. Revelation 1:15 says, *"...and His voice thundered like mighty ocean waves"* (NLT). The KJV says His voice is like the sound of many waters. What this means is that His voice will ultimately win out over all the other voices out there.

If your heart motive stays right and you are committed to the Lord, you will hear Him. That is because His voice cannot be missed. When you stand on the beach near the ocean, you don't miss the sound of the crashing waves rolling ashore. When you stand near the Lord and stay close to Him in your heart, you won't miss the unique and loud sound of His voice.

The reason we often miss the loudness of His voice is because we get too far away. We get too busy with daily activities, jobs, and various distractions until we realize that we aren't as close to God as we should be.

If you stay pressed in to Him in prayer and devotion, you will start to hear His roar! Once that happens, you become familiar with how God sounds to you.

For each person His voice will sound slightly different because we are all different. But what is the same is that God's voice according to Scripture has the element of force and loudness. More than once the Bible says His voice sounds like crashing waves (see Ps. 93:4). It is also described as thunder, and God even says of Himself that He will roar like a man of war (see Isa. 42:13).

I have found that praying in the Spirit causes the loudness of His voice to increase. Look at Psalm 29:3, which says, *"The voice of the Lord is upon the waters: the God of glory thundereth: the Lord is upon many waters."* Where does this verse say we find God's voice? It is found on the waters. Jesus said in John 7:38-39:

> *He that believeth on Me...out of his belly shall flow rivers of living water. (But this spake He of the Spirit, which they that believe on Him should receive...).*

When you pray in tongues, it is like rivers of waters coming out of you, and the voice of the Lord is found on those waters! The more you do it, the more pronounced the sound of His voice will become. As you are presented in life with lots of input and advice from all sides, remember to revert back to praying in the Spirit. This will cause God's voice to dominate the others and gradually eliminate those influences that are not of Him.

You will find yourself less easily moved by all the chatter of the world around you and even less confused by the things that sound good but may not be from God. Praying in the Spirit will also shed light on the advice of family, friends, and pastors that is from God. The things that are from God will begin to stand out to you.

The wonderful thing about praying in the Spirit is that it is supernatural. As you are trying to hear God and make decisions every day in line with His will, praying in tongues can cover all of them simultaneously. You may find that it won't take as long for you to sort out all the "God things" when you pray in the Spirit. When you add this supernatural dimension, things begin to just snap into place, and you find yourself operating above human limitations.

I like to think of praying in tongues like the difference between riding in a car and flying in an airplane. Sure, air travel isn't required for every little commute, but at times you have to cover a lot of ground in a short amount of time. You need to bypass all the obstacles on the ground and just get there!

You need lifestyle principles for following God's will, which is like driving your car every day. If you don't have these principles you will not be well-rounded and developed in your walk with God. After that, you need the addition of praying in tongues, which is like flying in an airplane. It gets you there faster and bypasses human limitations. It's the supernatural element to tapping into the heart and mind of God, and it covers a lot of ground that would have otherwise overwhelmed you.

STAY WITH THE RIGHT SOURCES

One reason we get overwhelmed by too much outside input is we open ourselves to too much of it. One of the biggest culprits to this problem is media resources. We are a generation inundated by these influences. Every day we are connected online via our computers, phones, and media gadgets. We have televisions in multiple rooms of our houses. It's no wonder people struggle to make sense of it all because the volume is more than we need to be subjecting ourselves to.

Something as simple as a radio advertisement can get you off track in making right choices in following the Lord. You are riding to work and hear a new scientific finding from recent research on health risks for those over a certain age. You realize that group mentioned applies to you, and therefore, the rest of the day you find yourself stewing about all the health risks you probably have. Something like this can misdirect you from following God accurately.

You will do yourself a great favor by eliminating many resources. This isn't to say there isn't good and helpful information online, but use prudence. Otherwise, you may find that you have added so much input that you will find it hard to hear God. Or when you do hear Him, you will be apt not to follow because of these other things.

As you absorb different pieces of information in following God, be sure to stay with the right sources. Pray, read your Bible, and listen to trustworthy people. Avoid carnal people, along with the excess secular advice coming from the media world. Sometimes it isn't that you need to weigh out all the voices and influences; some you just need to eliminate altogether. Keep outside sources limited to the right ones, and this will make listening to the Lord less of a challenge.

I have known many Christian people who listen to all the wrong sources. They will listen to the television preacher over their pastor who knows them. They will heed some advertisement over godly counsel or spend money on a get-rich-quick scheme rather than just buckle down to wise money management. In the end, their actions could probably be traced back to wrong heart motives that drive some people to seek all these things.

However, staying with the right, trustworthy sources will scale down the potential for the wrong input. It's less of a hassle because there isn't so much to sort through. You have to eliminate the baggage.

As you learn to seek God's will among the many voices and input out there, realize that God's ability to communicate above all of them is certain. If you will commit your will to Him and make some right decisions, rest assured His voice will win out over the rest!

Chapter Seven

HEARING GOD IN THE MIDST OF BLINDING EMOTIONS

Do not fret or have any anxiety about anything, but in every circumstance and in everything, by prayer and petition (definite requests), with thanksgiving, continue to make your wants known to God (Philippians 4:6 AMP).

Calmly and quietly, I drove with my son to the emergency room assuring him there was nothing to worry about. I must admit, a lump tried to enter my throat because I knew something wasn't right. I recognized the same symptoms from another relative of ours so I knew it was serious.

I rehearsed in my mind the words of a famous preacher that I had heard over 20 years ago. He talked about a time of crisis when he got a call that a family member was critical in the hospital. Rather than react frantically, the preacher said aloud to himself, "Faith is never desperate!" I reminded myself of this principle and remained calm as we drove down the street.

Earlier that day, I had told my husband that I felt I needed to take our 10-year-old son to the doctor because I noticed an unmistakable sweet odor on his breath, along with some other symptoms. I walked into our son's bedroom and asked him to put on his shoes because I wanted the doctor to check him out. He kept asking why, and I just remember saying, "I think some of the things you have been dealing with lately need to get checked out." He said, "What do you think it is, Mom?" I told him that we would have the doctor decide, but I knew what it was. I recognized the symptoms of diabetes, a disease with no known cure.

Also, during the same period of time, three other of our near relatives were diagnosed with some stage of cancer. At the time, some were not Christians and needed salvation. Another relative, whom we knew wasn't committed to the Lord, tried to commit suicide several times. It felt like a time of crisis.

When we left the hospital with our son, after the confirmed diagnosis of type 1 diabetes, we were suddenly in a tailspin trying to redesign our already busy lives to manage it. Everything about our daily routine would need to be adjusted. We also had to walk our son through his own emotions and help him understand what this all meant.

The next morning we went to the doctor in order to get him set up on insulin injections. The night before at the ER, our son was in terror of needles. He was less upset by the diabetes itself and more in terror of the IV getting put into his arm! He hates needles! However, Jon is a warrior in spirit. He has one of those personalities that isn't afraid to confront anything.

So when he learned that he would have to take daily injections, fighting past tears, he said, "OK, Mom. I will give myself this shot if you give me twenty-five bucks!" So 25 bucks it was! Then he bravely grabbed his first injection and stuck himself and said, "Yep, I did it!" A kid who was terrified of all needles the day prior just looked the situation square in the eye and decided to win. He has reacted the same way ever since.

My husband and I walked through this determined to be winners in the spirit too. I can remember the first few days feeling fear trying to hit me because of all the unknowns. As a family, we did what we knew to do, we confronted the unknowns with faith, and we kept our heads soundly in the game.

That is when God began to speak. We all began to receive different revelations and dreams about things pertaining to Jon's future. We got calls and prophecies from different ones around the nation who were able to speak into Jon's life. We began to fight for Jon's healing according to the Word of God. Although the healing has been a process, we are confident Jon will ultimately stand among those who have been healed by the power of God. Many miracles continue to take place in him.

Of our other relatives dealing with cancer, two were given a cancer-free report, and the third person got saved. I believe our progression to victory was because we stood our ground with God in the midst of crisis. We didn't freak out, but instead we took control of our emotions and began to look for His voice.

SETTLE DOWN

One of the main reasons people struggle to find the will of God during a time of crisis is because they are too worked up. Their emotions are blinding them from seeing and hearing God. In Mark 5:23, when Jairus came to Jesus because his daughter was dying, he was so desperate that he requested Jesus to come heal his daughter in a forceful way. The Bible says that Jairus *"besought"* Jesus. This means that he was applying extreme pressure to make it happen. He didn't even ask Jesus to come in the form of a cordial request. His words almost sounded like an order as he demanded Jesus come to His house.

Now let me interject a point here. It wasn't hard to get Jesus to respond to his request. We have to realize that when we are in a crisis, the Lord is ready to act on our behalf. The reason we often struggle to see that is because we are so worked up and responding to what we are facing as if we don't believe it.

Some time ago, after a service where we were ministering, I prayed for a lady who had just been notified that her home was going into foreclosure. She came begging for prayer. I remember encouraging her that we serve the God of the impossible and that no matter what, God was at work for her and she would come through this in total blessing. That seemed to encourage her spirits and calm her down. After we got home, I told my husband about the woman I prayed for. He said, "Really? I prayed for the same lady; she was so upset and in tears!" I put two and two together and realized that after I prayed with her, she got worked up again and went to somebody else! She had a hard time coming to peace on it.

Jairus must have had a similar struggle. As he and Jesus were nearing his house, several people came to meet them saying, "Don't bother coming now; she is dead!" Jesus must have seen the terror return to Jairus' face and immediately told him not to quit believing (see Mark 5:35-36). Jesus didn't want him to get worked up again, which would hinder his faith.

You probably recall how the story goes: When they arrived at the house they were greeted by a troop of mourners and people crying loudly. Emotions and desperation at the scene were at an all time high.

Jesus' response to their commotion was, *"Why make ye this ado, and weep? The damsel is not dead, but sleepeth"* (Mark 5:39). They all thought Jesus had lost His mind and began to laugh and mock Him. Although the Bible doesn't say it, I also suspect people thought His response was a bit harsh and inconsiderate because that is how people often respond today when you try and get them to keep their emotions in check.

Jesus was trying to get them all to calm down so He could create an environment conducive for a miracle. When they wouldn't do it, Jesus had to ask them to leave the room. When we are too worked up emotionally during a time of crisis, we often close our ears to the voice of the Lord when He wants to help us. The reason Jesus didn't want Jairus to get worked up was because it would have prevented him from focusing on the miracle at hand.

When a time of crisis is upon you, make a decision to keep your head together. I know that sometimes human nature is to react or feel a sense of anxiety. However, when you allow your emotions to remain at the forefront, it really sends the message to yourself and others that you aren't confident that God is there to come through.

A few years ago, a couple in our church shared a powerful healing testimony. One night the husband had not been acting right and was struggling to talk and form words. The wife took him to the doctor, and they discovered that he had had a mini-stroke. When the diagnosis came, they didn't get upset.

They prayed and said, "Lord, we are tithers and we have tither's rights! Therefore, we know that the devourer is rebuked for us, and we expect total healing!"

They determined to stay level-headed and expect his healing to manifest. Several months later, they went back to the doctor for a follow-up test. The doctor was amazed. Expecting to find remnant scarring from the episode, he was shocked to find no evidence that a stroke had ever happened. They kept their heads in the midst of the crisis, which enabled them to follow God's will for a complete healing.

AVOID THE COMMOTION

My mother is a very caring person, but she has never been one to get freaked out or down about much of anything. She takes what life throws at her with a laugh. Even in our toughest times growing up, she would always push us to face our fears by saying, "Oh now, just go on and do it!" That's how we forged into new schools, first job interviews, and the multifaceted world of the unknowns. Her attitude has always been to forge on and face whatever is before her.

To this day, I thank her for putting that in us because, in many a crisis, I have avoided getting caught up in the commotion of it. It has kept me level-headed and in faith, feeling like I can conquer anything with God.

To this day, that is often how I counsel people. I try to keep people from some kind of excessive emotional response. I avoid too much crying with them, not because I don't have a heart-felt compassion for the things people go through. I know how painful some of the struggles of life can be, and some human emotion is normal and understandable. At the same time, I also know that emotion won't fix the issue. What I want to do is help people get past the emotional response so they can focus on hearing God for the wisdom and the answer.

I know that if you want to hear God's voice in the middle of a situation, you simply can't get caught up in the commotion of it. Creating a scene will not change a thing! It will only make you feel worse and get everyone else involved in fear. It will not cause God to respond any faster, so why do it? Out of love, I try to push people to avoid this tendency. Making a commotion like the family did at the house of Jairus will only hinder the power of God and possibly cause you to make some bad decisions outside His will.

Some people grew up in families that created commotion. It's all they know. They can hardly do anything without their feelings being at the forefront. They are easily jostled back and forth by the storms of life. When they come to church, you can tell what kind of day they had. They wear their expressions on their faces. And they want you and others to notice.

Some of the things they are upset by aren't as big as they are making them, but they have trained themselves to respond to life with emotion and commotion. They make such a habit of this that they turn every little thing into a big deal. They respond to things by phoning anyone and everyone, and they get everyone worked up.

Those who do this sort of thing don't realize that they are attracting more crisis to themselves. Remember, demons look for any opportunity to find a way in, and wrong words, fear, and runaway emotions are just the ticket they need.

When Jesus came upon the commotion at the house of Jairus, He had to separate Himself from it. He put the commotion-makers out of the house so they wouldn't interrupt the miracle.

By quieting the commotion, you enable God to speak. With some people, God can't get a word in edgewise because they are making too big of a scene. Without calming down and staying in the spirit, you may miss the voice of the Lord trying to give you the answer.

In Luke 21:19, Jesus said, *"In your patience possess ye your souls."* The word patience here means "committed endurance." In other words, possessing our souls will take some effort because runaway emotions try to surface in all of us when a crisis is upon us. They will press upon us in such a way that we feel we are going to crumble underneath them. They want to keep returning as we walk through the situation with the Lord. The Lord is telling us in this verse to take control of these kinds of emotions. The word possess here means "to own." We could rephrase this verse, "With committed endurance, own and stay in control of your own mind." We have to make our minds and emotions calm down and conform to us.

The time when you need to hear God most is during a crisis, but if you get worked up, you risk not hearing Him speak. Perhaps you lost your job and don't know how you are going to pay the bills, or a family member is away from God and making dangerous lifestyle choices. At such times you begin to think desperately of all the things you could or should do. Letting the voice of the Lord begin to come through requires you to calm your head and emotions.

THE STRONGHOLD OF FEAR

Never forget that fear is a demon. It will try to manifest during times of crisis. Fear has many different manifestations. It can appear as stress, fret, worry, nervousness, anxiety, phobias, and terror. For some people, it manifests as a night terror in the form of bad dreams and nightmares. Psalm 91:5 says that there is a terror that comes specifically at night.

The Bible speaks a lot about the power of fear, and we find countless Scriptures that use the phrase "fear not" (see Gen. 15:1; 26:24; Deut. 31:8; Matt. 28:5; Luke 1:30; 2:10; 12:32; John 12:15). The Lord must have known that this would be a common human tendency. If we don't address fear, it will increase and potentially pull us out of the will of God. That is because we will start adjusting our lives around it.

For example, people who have financial fears and phobias, even if they are very wealthy, can become stingy and hoard their money. They are so afraid something terrible will happen to their money that they don't want to tithe or give offerings into the Kingdom of God. Even though God wants them to do these things, they miss God's will and plan all because of fear.

When you are in a crisis or even if you just feel like fear is trying to grip your life in some way, deal with it. Identify what it is and command the demon of fear to leave you in Jesus' name! If you have put up with it for a long time, you may have to keep standing your ground so it cannot return. Perhaps you can make some lifestyle changes in order to retrain yourself from reverting back to the habit of fear. Don't allow some form of fear to keep you imprisoned until you can't follow and obey the will of God for your life.

TODAY'S CHOICES: TOMORROW'S HABITS

One of the biggest struggles people have when it comes to finding God's will during a time of crisis is the fact that the situation doesn't always allow them ample time to think and come up with the appropriate response. Some are emergency situations that demand immediate decisions. This isn't the time to declare a fast and an extended period of prayer in order to wait on God for an answer! There isn't time for it.

So how do you hear from God on a moment's notice when you just don't have time to quiet down and wait? Although it's not a new answer, there is really only one answer: Prepare yourself ahead of time. You decide every day to do what the Bible says and build "your house" to withstand a storm. Jesus taught this principle in Matthew 7:24-27. He said that whoever makes the continual decision to do what God says according to the Bible will be like a wise man whose house will withstand the storms of life.

The reason this principle is so powerful is that it causes you to build a habit. Today's choices are tomorrow's habits. As you steadily make the right choices to follow God and obey His Word each day, you are preparing yourself to respond instantly and accurately when a crisis comes. You won't have to sit and wonder if you are making the right decision; you will automatically respond in line with what you have been putting inside you every day. You will simply do what you have "practiced."

SUPERNATURAL WISDOM

I once heard a preacher say, "Even when you don't think you know what to do, always respond in faith, saying to yourself, 'I know what to do!'" Why can you say that? It is because you walk with the God of all wisdom who will cause you to know what to do even in the most challenging crisis.

James 1:2-8 talks about asking God for wisdom. I believe the wisdom this passage is referring to is special wisdom needed during a time of trial or crisis. That is why verses 2-3 say: *"Count it all joy when ye fall into divers temptations; knowing this, that the trying of your faith worketh patience."* Then the rest of the passage talks about how to obtain wisdom from God during these challenges.

God has designated special and supernatural wisdom for any crisis we can face. This means His will and guidance are available at a moment's notice. All we have to do is know how to obtain them. Look at verses 5-8:

> *If any of you lack wisdom, let him ask of God, that giveth to all men liberally, and upbraideth not; and it shall be given him. But let him ask in faith, nothing wavering. For he that wavereth is like a wave of the sea driven with the wind and tossed. For let not that man think that he shall receive anything of the Lord. A double minded man is unstable in all his ways* (James 1:5-8).

So how do we obtain this kind of supernatural wisdom? It requires two things. First, we have to ask God for it. Second, we have to expect it to manifest. In other words, once we ask God to give the wisdom, we need to act and respond like we have received it. Like the preacher I mentioned above said, "I know what to do!"

We will be tested as to whether or not we truly believe that sometimes. Sure, when the storms of life are blowing hard, our situations may make us feel like we are going to blow away with them! It may not seem like the wisdom is coming, but no matter what, we have to stand there in faith and be determined that wisdom and guidance are there. When we do, we won't blow away with the storm; we will stand firm. But as the passage says, if we start to guess and wonder if God is there guiding us, we will be tossed into the waves.

As you listen and follow God's will during a time of crisis, keep your head together, pull back, and listen to God no matter how tempting it is to get all worked up. If you are having to make some fast decisions, be at peace, knowing that if you have been doing the right things, you will respond with God like it's second nature. Lastly, never feel reserved about calling on God for an extra dose of supernatural wisdom. God is ready to give wisdom for whatever it is you are walking through today. Have faith that it's there no matter what you are dealing with. Whether you face a financial situation, a family issue, a work-related challenge, or a health concern (like diabetes in our case), you will come out of it in victory, fully in line with God's divine will!

Chapter Eight

FINDING GOD'S WILL FOR BUSINESS, OCCUPATION, AND MONEY

...Let the Lord be magnified, which hath pleasure in the prosperity of His servant **(Psalm 35:27).**

One of the biggest struggles many Christians have is finding God's will not only for choosing a career path, but also in finding and choosing the right job. Everyone needs profitable employment. We know that the Bible says in Second Thessalonians 3:10, *"For even when we were with you, this we commanded you, that if any would not work, neither should he eat."* This means that every household should have consistent, reliable income so that the members of the family are well supplied and able to be a financial blessing in the Kingdom of God as well.

Still there are plenty of well-meaning Christians who never seem to find their niche when it comes to some kind of career path, or they have trouble staying gainfully employed. Others stay employed, but struggle to become settled and can't seem to progress into some measure of occupational and financial stability. A third group just want to know if the career direction or a certain job they are pursuing is what God wants for them.

I don't think it is God's intention for Christians to bounce around from one job to the next or one new business venture to the next and never become settled in anything. Twenty years into adulthood, some people are no further along in life than they were out of high school. God has a purpose for you and He wants you to be set on that path to the point that you feel you are doing something purposeful with your life.

WHAT AM I CALLED TO DO?

Determining a career path isn't always easy. Even if you know what your plans are, often a process is required to get there. My encouragement in locating God's will for your career path is to first put the larger principles for finding God's will, which we have previously discussed, into practice. Then begin to locate several factors that will help open your eyes to God's will regarding your occupational purpose in life.

LOOK FOR YOUR HEART'S DESIRE

As a teenager, I wanted to go into full-time ministry. It was all I could think of, and the desire for it never left me. In spite of attending a Christian high school that didn't believe in women preachers and not having any real options for ministry before me, I never quit wanting it. I remember using my mother's ironing board as a pretend pulpit in my bedroom as I imagined preaching

God's Word. When I graduated from high school, no options for Spirit-filled, full-time ministry positions were waiting for me. I looked into Bible school, but our family was unable to afford it at the time, so that wasn't an immediate option.

In the meantime, I had to do something with my life. I couldn't just wait around indefinitely for ministry to come my way. I got a part-time job and stayed very involved in my church. I had some great opportunities given me to minister in my local church and gained an incredible amount of training there, but there were no full-time positions open. I took a full-time job at a bank and began to take evening classes in accounting because my job had a program to pay for them. I figured that I needed to be doing something constructive toward my future regardless of my desire for ministry.

Two years later, my church offered me a job, and I eventually became the assistant bookkeeper. Even when full-time ministry wasn't available, my accounting classes proved useful and helped launch me into what was to be the beginning of my future in ministry. Working at the church, I met my husband. He was an intern at the church, also pursuing full-time ministry. We got married, and both of us pursued ministry through what would prove to be a long process that ultimately brought us to where we are today.

What I want you to see is that even though I became a bookkeeper and worked other jobs, I never quit loving the ministry. I never lost my desire to preach even though it took years for it to come to fruition. Among other things, the one main ingredient that solidified in me what I was to do in life was that preaching and ministry burned in my heart.

Not everyone is called to full-time ministry, yet the principle for finding your full-time purpose is the same. Often the thing you can't get away from is the very thing you are supposed to do. God will drop things in your heart, and they will stay with you. However, most of the time, not every detail on how you will get there is clear. Although ministry burned in my heart from my youth, for many years I had no idea that it would one day include pastoring a church, among other responsibilities.

The key is, look for one area that burns in your heart. Those desires are often there because God put them there. As long as you are pursuing the Lord wholeheartedly, those desires will be the proper ones and won't be tainted by the wrong motives and influences.

You might be saying, "I just don't know what burns in me! In fact, what I am doing today seemed like a good idea at the time, but I don't know if it was the right choice." Well, if you are unsettled with it, you may want to pray and ask the Lord to reveal the right path. Some parts of your God-breathed destiny won't be revealed or manifest until later in your life. Allow the Lord to drop something in your heart that you are fulfilled in doing. Usually, if you dig deep enough, you will find something that you are drawn to or feel that God wants for you.

FOLLOW THE PROCESS THROUGH

Once you get set on a path, realize there is a process to get there. Most people get disillusioned because they never let the process play out. They get all excited about something, rush into it, and completely forget that nothing pays off overnight.

There are no shortcuts or easy paths if you are going to pursue a long-term, profitable occupational path. Most things take years to become stable and successful.

Some people never get to the stage where they begin to experience results. Either they don't finish their degrees or they don't stick with the hard work necessary. They aren't willing to take less-than-desirable jobs in the interim. They aren't willing to go through the investment years that promise little to no profit while they feel like they are living on just peanut butter for food!

I have known many people, even good Christians, who get excited about something they want to do with their lives. They commonly jump out and start a new business or some kind of ministry without thinking through the long-term demands this effort is going to require. They don't consider that many years may come and go before any real profit or fruit is seen.

I can testify of this when it comes to ministry. Our ministry has only really begun to bear some very visible fruit and growth in the last several years prior to this book. We have been in full-time ministry for years, but we had to work it step by step and not quit when things weren't always going just as we had hoped.

This is commonly why people jump from thing to thing and don't stick with anything. They want instant results and don't want to work the process or develop their skills or knowledge base. They don't have the patience to see something through that may take many years to become what they wanted it to be. So they jump from thing to thing, hoping the long process or leaner years won't be necessary.

MAKING A DECISION ON A JOB

As we follow the process into our future destiny, we all have to make money in the meantime! We have to put a roof over our heads, have food to eat, support a family, and so forth. I understand that for most people several interim steps are necessary to get where God wants them.

I not only worked at one bank prior to ministry, I worked at two. After my husband and I were married, we were struggling to make ends meet while traveling in ministry. We both got other secular jobs rather than not be able to pay the bills. It wasn't what we wanted to do, but it was what we had to do until God caused our ministry to grow.

If you are praying for God's will regarding a certain job, again, use the basic principles for finding God's will and always listen to God in your spirit. In addition to that, consider several factors as you listen to the Lord. Most of them that I have listed here are simple common sense principles, but if you take each into account you will be better prepared to take the right employment path.

GAINFUL EMPLOYMENT

Decide if the job being considered will meet your needs. I know people who take jobs that don't get the bills paid. Now that isn't to say you shouldn't take a job in the meantime till you find something that does. A little money is better than none at all! Yet, some people sit at the same jobs year after year knowing they aren't supplying enough for their families. They have no drive or vision for something better.

Perhaps, like Abraham and Isaac, if a famine is in the land, you need to get creative or get yourself moving to someplace that will supply for you (see Gen. 12:10; 26:12,18) just to make ends meet until you are able to step into what God ultimately wants for your life. Don't just wander aimlessly for months and years in jobs that aren't getting the bills paid.

GODLY EMPLOYMENT

I know some Christians who take certain jobs that pay well, but the problem is the type of work isn't conducive to the Bible and Christian living. They take jobs that ask them to use shady or high pressure sales tactics. They work in industries that do not represent Christianity correctly. For example, I personally don't think any virtuous woman needs to be parading on stage in skimpy swimwear in the name of fashion modeling. For the job to line up with God's will, it needs to be in line with biblical principles and needs to represent Christian conduct.

FAMILY-CONDUCIVE EMPLOYMENT

Some don't consider their family responsibilities when choosing a job. They will work all kinds of odd hours so their spouses and children hardly see them. The kids get home from school when the parent is already gone to work, and the parent doesn't get home till after the kids are in bed. The same schedule goes on for weeks, months, and years. God doesn't want your family to permanently suffer because of a job that prevents you from having any normal home life. This plan may be OK for a short period of time, but think of the long term effects on your family and personal time.

KINGDOM-CONDUCIVE EMPLOYMENT

Some people take jobs that keep them perpetually out of church. Now I understand some lines of work don't call for weekday, daytime hours. For example, doctors often have to put in unusual or unexpected hours. However, you need to make sure God and church involvement are able to be a priority in any position or career path you take. If the job or position will keep you from church services on an ongoing basis, perhaps it isn't the best option.

I know countless Christians who ignore this, and their lives suffer terribly from it. They move across the globe for some big job they think will catapult them into success, but they don't even consider any form of local church commitment while considering the move. Personally, I wouldn't move anywhere to take a job if there wasn't a powerful church there that I could get involved in for some eternal purpose. I would consider that before all else. In fact, I know many Christians who take the same stance as I do, and they aren't even called to full-time ministry. They put their church calling first over their earthly job options because they want God to use them for a higher, more eternal purpose than just getting ahead in life financially.

Lastly, I can't say enough about listening to your spirit when it comes to choosing any job or position. Really it's true with anything in life. If something deep in your heart gives you a cautious feeling that you can't get away from, it's probably the Holy Spirit telling you that this job isn't for you.

OCCUPATIONAL SUCCESS STARTS HERE

As we pursue God's will for handling our occupations, businesses, and even our money, we can be in the right place, but end up unsuccessful if certain principles are forgotten, so let's cover them briefly here. In other words, we can be in God's will concerning our direction, but never obtain the intended results.

ETHICS AND INTEGRITY

You cannot ignore the need for integrity and the need to deal with people properly according the Bible. I am sure you are like me and have met people in churches who lie, steal, and swindle people in the church while they lift their hands in praise. Then they make their bad practices all sound really good, like there was nothing shady about them.

We can't live on the edge of compromise and expect to prosper because we reap what we sow (see Gal. 6:7). If we are sneaky and untruthful about our business habits and we take advantage of others by not paying them monies owed them, we can't expect to stay blessed. Some people think nothing of using manipulative tactics to get other church members to feel sorry for them so they will give them money. Rather than work hard, trust God, and put biblical principles into practice, they will shortchange a Christian brother or sister.

It is also wrong to go out and spend "fun" money when you can't pay your bills, yet people do it all the time. You shouldn't go on a vacation and to the movies when you can't pay your mortgage or electric bill. Psalm 25:21 says, *"Let integrity and uprightness preserve me; for I wait on Thee."* What will preserve you? Integrity and the decision to do what is right, no matter what.

STEWARDSHIP AND MANAGEMENT

Some never come into God's will and blessing because of bad stewardship and management. Let me begin by saying that I wouldn't begin a business venture or even a ministry unless I had the proven management skills to make it successful. This doesn't mean you need to have a business management degree to start a business. However, if you can't even manage your own finances or keep a schedule and a clean home, then perhaps those same problems will prevent you from proper business or ministry management. I know people who start businesses because of good ideas and even personal talents, gifts, and skills, but they don't have the business management or perhaps even marketing skills to cause the business to succeed.

Some people can't seem to succeed because they have never learned the discipline or developed skills to manage money, or countless other things for that matter. Someone could be smack in the middle of God's will but miss His best because of their lack of good stewardship! This is an all-too-common tragedy in the Kingdom of God.

I encourage you to work on your management skills when it comes to organization and stewardship of money, regardless of what business you are in. In First Timothy 1:12, Paul said, *"And I thank Christ Jesus our Lord, who hath enabled me, for that He counted me faithful, putting me into the ministry."* Although full-time ministry was God's will for Paul, he wouldn't have been able to embrace or even walk in the call if God hadn't seen his faithfulness and good stewardship over what was entrusted to him.

I know people who exhibit a real heart for God and even a call to ministry, but they never get there because they can't manage money, a schedule, or even themselves in a way that properly represents the Kingdom of God. Don't miss God's destiny for your life because of bad personal life management and stewardship over what God has entrusted to you.

CONSISTENCY

Nothing will succeed without consistency. You can be called, and you can be as talented and gifted as they come, but if you aren't consistent, you will never reach your full potential. This happened with the children of Israel. God had a call for them. His will was the Promised Land, but their inconsistency caused many of them to die off in the wilderness and miss what God ultimately had for them. They missed His will because they were in and out of things. They were on one day and off the next. One day they were strong with God, and the next day they backslid (see Exod. 15:21-24; Ps. 106:12-14).

Some people can't even be consistent to make their beds in the morning or remember to keep their cars full of gasoline. They are late to most every appointment and never remember to pay bills. Some aren't on top of their personal hygiene or manners and social skills. You can't be inconsistent in your life, going in and out of sin, tithing then non-tithing, keeping a schedule one day and not the next, and expect to fulfill God's will for you.

Think about it. Those who graduate with a degree in some field did so because they worked until they obtained. Keep yourself consistent, not only with the practical and work requirements of life, but also in your private walk with God. This kind of discipline and willingness to keep progressing will promote you!

GOD'S WILL FOR PROSPERITY AND MONEY

This isn't a book about biblical prosperity, so we won't spend time teaching all the principles on it here. However, because the subject is often debated, we do need to know whether or not God wants us to prosper financially as part of His will for business and occupational pursuits.

Some think God wants us to live with little to nothing because that somehow represents humility. That thought, however, would go against too many biblical examples where God blessed and prospered His people, not just spiritually and physically, but also materially. In fact, Psalm 35:27 says, *"...let the Lord be magnified, which hath pleasure in the prosperity of His servant."* Some translations, such as the NIV, say, *"well-being of His servant."* Really, that is what true prosperity is. It is having well-being in every area of life, which if we are to be honest, must include finances.

It's God's will for everyone to prosper. God isn't bound by money, but He also isn't offended by it or by those who have it. In fact, it takes money to preach the Gospel. We saw this both in the ministry of Jesus and that of the early apostles.

What we have to understand along the lines of prosperity is that prosperity in general will mean something different for everyone. It will often be different based on people's educational qualifications, priorities, occupational choices, and so forth. We can't erroneously think that because God wants us to prosper, money will start falling from the sky and it won't require a quality work ethic, gainful employment, or other important principles. Nor can we assume it means we must become the next face on the Forbes 400.

There is no doubt that God can and does put supernatural money into our hands. I am one who can attest to the truth of this. We have been given cars, clothes, and countless other material things, and not because we were some famous ministry personalities. These things came along when we were working secular jobs and just trying to find some stable place in the ministry.

However, I will say we used our faith and always expected to see God's blessing come our way. When we have needed cars or houses, we were confident that God would supply. Still, we worked our jobs and did the best we could with our very limited educational strengths at the time. We tithed, gave sacrificial offerings, paid our bills, and did our best to manage our money correctly. From there, God blessed us in ways we would have never seen coming, and we could never have pulled them off on our own, no matter how hard we worked or tweaked the budget! God has always given us more than we could have imagined in all the years we have known and served Him.

What anyone of us can't do is define prosperity by someone else's measuring stick. We can't determine it based on someone's material possessions or lack thereof. Some people's material possessions don't make them appear prosperous at all, but they may have countless thousands hidden in the bank. Others have all sorts of material things, gadgets, and toys but are hopelessly in dangerous debt.

God wants to paint your own personal portfolio of supernatural prosperity that will include certain provision for needs and even many personal wants so that you can live a satisfied life. This doesn't mean that God can't or won't make you independently wealthy. I certainly can't say He won't because it happens! We see this both in the Bible and in our present day. God has given His people witty ideas, inventions, and investments that evolved into very prosperous ventures that shocked everyone because the ones it happened to didn't appear qualified for such a thing.

However, what we really need to focus on is that God wants us blessed and that the measure of blessing may be different for different people, depending on any number of variables. The key is that with God it can be beyond our ability. Our job is to do what is needed so that God can bless us supernaturally. God blessed Abraham, but there were several things Abraham did that positioned him for God's prosperity. If we do the same, God will prosper us as well.

1. *Work an occupational skill or job.* Although God prospered Abraham beyond human

comprehension, Abraham was also a hard worker and business manager. He managed several hundred servants and livestock (see Gen. 13:2; 14:14) and dug several irrigation wells (see Gen. 21:30; 26:18).

2. *Tithe and give offerings.* Abraham was a tither (see Gen. 14:20), and he offered to God sacrificially. He even gave his own son, Isaac (see Gen. 22).

3. *Use proper stewardship with what is given you.* When Abraham and Lot couldn't economically share the same land, Abraham made a wise business decision for them to choose key separate pieces of property (see Gen. 13:6-12). He also wisely secured the safety of his wells with King Abimelech (see Gen. 21:25-32).

4. *Have faith.* Abraham believed God would do what He promised. God promised to prosper him and make him the father of many nations, and in spite of some challenging circumstances, Abraham believed God's words to him (see Gen. 15:6; Rom. 4:3).

5. *Obey God and live in righteousness.* Abraham obeyed God's commands (see Gen. 12:1-4; 15:9-11). He commanded his children in righteousness (see Gen. 18:19) and continually called on the Lord (see Gen. 12:8; 13:4,18; 21:33).

So as we use our faith for God to prosper us, we need to stay with Scripture, find our occupational direction, and work it with diligence and obedience.

Feel confident today that God has a destiny for you. Even if you have made some mistakes in the areas we have discussed in this chapter, God will help you and work with you. Everyone has made mistakes! The Lord wants to help you find your path in life and get on top of things in the areas of business and money. You can trust that the Lord is there to hold you by the hand and help you find His will in these areas if you are willing to grow with Him (see Isa. 41:13).

Chapter Nine

FINDING GOD'S WILL IN RELATIONSHIPS, DATING, MARRIAGE, AND FAMILY

Do not be bound together with unbelievers; for what partnership have righteousness and lawlessness, or what fellowship has light with darkness? (2 Corinthians 6:14 NASB)

It is often said that choosing the right person to marry is one of the most important decisions anyone can make. This is so true. In fact, marrying the wrong person—one who doesn't share an individual's goals, values, or even spiritual pursuits—has been one of the greatest factors keeping people out of the will of God for years into their future.

Think about how many people have missed college opportunities because of bad marriages or because of wrong dating relationships. I know people in full-time ministry who have problems fulfilling their callings with God because of spouses who resist the ministry. Others have had to work through the hurt of horrible abuse because they married someone based on fleeting emotions. Of course, we can all think of someone, perhaps even ourselves, who wasted time on the wrong dating relationship. For some, not only was it a waste of time, but it caused a great deal of hurt feelings and often a host of other problems.

Of all the things that people should not get out of God's will on, dating and marriage are some of the most important because the results have such a lasting and permanent impact on people's lives. Yet, this area is one of most common places where people get out of God's will. Most Christians know the basic Bible principles about dating and marriage, and they know that they shouldn't date or marry a non-believer. However, many still do it and are sorry for it later. Other quality Christians just want to feel confident that if they do date or consider marrying someone, they can locate God's will on it.

Let me begin here by saying that it would be better to remain single and walk alone with God for the rest of your life than to marry the wrong person. Having counseled many people through dysfunctional marriages and families, I implore you not to marry the wrong person! Ask anyone who has been the victim of spousal abuse, irresponsibility, neglect, control and manipulation, financial ruin, or criminal issues, all because of a spouse.

This isn't to make people become fearful of getting married; it's meant to help people use godly wisdom that is conducive to following God's will.

Over the years, I have encountered many people who talk about how weary they are of waiting for Mr. or Miss Right to come along. After years of waiting, they begin to think that perfect person will never show up. Of course, usually prior to that, they started out with a list of qualifications for the spouse they wanted God to bring them. Often their list includes a fairly large number of godly character traits that they wanted the person to have.

As years go by, some begin to believe that their previous expectations were too high, so they settle for a few things less. Their expectations keep lowering, and as the years go by, some abandon the list altogether.

The devil watches this and, at the perfect moment, sends some "swanky" person of the opposite sex to their church. I mean, church is the place people want to meet their mate, right? So it all sounds really good! Of course, for some the devil doesn't even have to bring the person to church; the compromising Christian goes looking for possible dates in places they shouldn't.

So the devil has this new potential candidate waltz in at the "perfect" moment because by now these good Christians are so desperate for a mate that they start to look for creative reasons why this person fits the bill. Ignore the fact that the new potential candidate doesn't have consistent income or has been married multiple times. Ignore that he (or she) can't lift his hands in praise or connect to the pastor's message.

Although this individual doesn't pass most of the qualifications on the original list of expectations for a spouse, by now these Christians are reasoning past countless warning signs. Then too often, in spite of concerns from friends, family, and pastoral counsel, they marry anyhow. We have all seen too many sad outcomes from this scenario when the formerly faithful Christians quit church, have their lives shattered, and even sometimes go back to serving the world altogether. Sadly, some just give in to living a compromised version of Christianity.

For those who truly want the will of God regarding someone to marry, there are several principles that they must hold dear. And they must make the sound decision that they will not compromise these principles. Let's review some key principles here for determining God's will for a mate.

THE PATTERN

The Bible says that marriage is a picture of Jesus and the Church. We know from Ephesians 5:22-33 that the husband represents Jesus, who is to love and take care of his wife. He is to be a spiritual example the way Jesus is to us. He is also to exhibit tenderness to his wife the same way Jesus does to the Body of Christ. The wife is then to reciprocate that tenderness and care with a giving and submissive spirit the way the Body of Christ respects Jesus. Remember the Body of Christ submits to Christ because of His love and provision. The wife is then to honor the husband the way the Church honors Christ and is dedicated to Him.

This is the most basic biblical pattern for marriage. The first key principle for finding the right person is to ask yourself, "Is the person I am dating or considering for marriage the kind of person with whom I will be able to emulate this pattern?" You need to determine if, should you marry each other, as a couple you will be able together to emulate Jesus and the Church.

Anyone who comes along can talk a good talk and act like a dedicated Christian. So you can't always go on how people present themselves initially. Additionally, even the best and most godly couples will be tested in their marriage relationships, so it pays to know in advance the character of the one you plan to marry. You need to make a sure determination ahead of time so that when your relationship in marriage is tested, you will still be confident that you are with the one God chose for you.

Therefore, it is wise to look at several factors that largely contribute to who many people are. Many of these factors are visible in who that person is today, but they can often be better located by considering who that person was before you met them. As you spend time together, keeping these factors in mind will help bring to the surface any areas of concern, or it will reassure you that this person is a good candidate for marriage.

A negative trait or two in some of the areas we are about to review doesn't automatically disqualify someone. We need to look for the person's overall character. But the smaller issues, especially if there are quite a few of them, often add up to who the person really is. If there is a concern, then the problem areas will usually become more pronounced, assuming we are willing to acknowledge them.

CHURCH INVOLVEMENT

Think about what the person's church involvement and experiences have been. Has this person been committed to church for a long time, or is the commitment intermittent? Someone who talks very little about church experience may not have had much. Maybe he or she has been in church but has been to three or four different churches in the last few years. Perhaps this person has a divisive, discontented spirit that causes church hopping. It may be good to consider whether this person tends to earn respect from fellow church members or the leadership in the overall church environment.

For some, it becomes clear that the potential mate's likes regarding church choices are different. Divided church interests have caused problems in many marriages! Also, consider how the person acts in church currently. Is the person attending church in an effort to have a real encounter with God, or is church attendance just a religious duty or experience? Does the person like going to church or enjoy talking about it? If the subject and interest of church seems far in the background all the time, it may be an area of concern.

CHRISTIAN EXPERIENCE

Is the person a committed Christian, exhibiting the basics for Christian maturity? A person who is an active, growing Christian will have fruit that is evident! It will be evident in how the person talks, prays, and treats other people. That person won't compromise or get you to compromise when no one is looking. Most people can tell a quality and stable Christian from one who isn't. The signs that there is a problem, again, will become evident if you are willing to see them.

FAMILY EXPERIENCE

Of course, more people than ever today grow up in dysfunctional families. You can't always determine what a person is like based on the family he or she comes from. However, if the person has been through several failed marriages, has siblings with failed marriages, and grew up without a father (and so forth), this is worth thinking over. Again, you can't always make it a determining factor. However, if he or she has a long string of family issues, either in the immediate family or near relatives, it is good to consider if the person has the life skills needed for being the kind of person you would want to start a family with. If this person came from a less-than-desirable family history, it is wise to ask yourself of he or she has developed the positive life skills needed to succeed beyond it.

SEXUAL EXPERIENCE

I realize that you may be considering marriage to someone who has been married before or who lived a troubled past but has truly experienced a total life transformation. There are quality people who cannot change their pasts. However, it is still a good idea to keep in mind that those who have come from a background with a lot of sexual problems and multiple experiences may not be able to respond correctly in that area in marriage.

Before marrying a person, you need to consider whether or not the problem has been healed or dealt with. In addition, a person who has limited conviction or self control regarding sex outside of marriage may not change their ways once married, and sometimes the problem worsens.

HOBBIES AND INTERESTS

A person's interests tell you a lot about him or her. What does your potential mate like to do on the weekends? Hopefully, the person's interests are pure and honorable, but if some are not, you need to consider how many more of the person's interests aren't honorable.

Also consider things such as a person having no hobbies because he or she is too busy working around the clock. This can also contribute to severe problems in marriage and family.

Does the person just want to engage in activities of his personal choosing, or is he interested in the activities of others? If the person only wants to focus on selfish interests, likes, comforts, and food choices, this will potentially escalate into further problems in the marriage years.

FRIENDSHIPS

As the old saying goes, "We are the company we keep." I have seen this in churches over and over. Mature, stable Christians tend to want to be around others who are the same. Carnal Christians tend to flock to other carnal Christians. Divisive and gossiping people like to hang with other gossipers.

I have been amazed at times when someone I have counseled with sexual problems will find someone else in the church whom we also counseled with similar sexual issues. The congregation may have no idea about the private lives of either of them. Yet we, knowing the problems both have had, watch them strike up a friendship with each other. I am not even saying the friendship is sexual in nature either. More often, it is just that these two "birds of the feather" so to speak tend to find one another and somehow become the newest "best of buddies."

In the same way, worldly people, even if they call themselves "Christians," will have worldly friends. They can try to explain all day long why this or that person is their friend, but if their friends don't have quality Christian fruit, there is nothing to explain. A person who constantly hangs with secular people or carnal and compromising Christians does so because something about those people relates to him or her.

Actually, the Bible has less to say about how to choose the right spouse than it does about how to choose the right friends. Of course, the biblical principles for choosing a mate are the same as those for choosing quality friends and should be held onto even more carefully. (See 1 Corinthians 5:11; 2 Thessalonians 3:6; James 4:4; 1 John 2:15; 2 John 10.)

FINANCIAL AND OCCUPATIONAL EXPERIENCE

People have said it for years, "Lady, if he doesn't have a job, don't marry him!" Does the person you are considering have a good work ethic? Can the person hold down a responsible job, or is the person gainfully employed? Even a woman planning to be a stay-at-home mother should have a strong work ethic to keep a clean home and care for the family's needs. Consider if the person has been able to remain on a job for a reasonable period of time. Personally, I see a concern when someone can't stick with anything and constantly bounces from job to job or from one fleeting business idea to another.

You should also consider a person's financial standards. Financial problems and credit disaster are one of the number one issues that destroy marriages. You usually don't have to hang around someone too long before you get some sense on where the person is, financially speaking. There are things that reveal financial stability, and there are usually telltale signs of problems or financial indiscretion. For example, if the person is constantly buying you lucrative gifts that you know the salary from his or her field of occupation can't typically afford, it may be a sign of concern.

LIFESTYLE AND CONVICTIONS

When considering someone for marriage, you have to look at overall lifestyle and personal convictions too. Some people don't think it's wrong to watch certain movies or go to the casino now and then. If you are going to marry someone, that person needs to share your biblical standards for living. If you are spending time together and you constantly struggle as to what activities are considered acceptable, this problem will only escalate later and will potentially create a vast division.

A person's lifestyle also has to do with cleanliness, hygiene, manners, and social graces. Sir, if you are always stopping by her apartment and the place has animals running all over and looks like a garbage dumpster, you better determine right now if that is the home you want to live in every day! Ma'am, if he tends to go around town unshaven, wearing a faded T-shirt, old cut-offs, and flip flops, then decide if that's who you want to be seen with at the mall. He may dress up for dates with you now, but when your everyday life together sets in, he may not be so dedicated to wearing presentable attire in public.

PERSONALITY

Lastly, you must decide if you are attracted to the potential mate's personality in general. Is the person enjoyable to be around? Does the person treat you right? Bouts of moodiness, tears, depression, anger, jealousy, silence, or touchiness won't just go away when you get married.

Pronounced or continually increasing areas of concern prior to marriage will not go away just because you tie the knot. Again look at the signs. The biggest reason why people miss God's best choice in a mate is because of the "love is blind" syndrome, which causes them ignore key signs. Most Christians who have any basic discernment typically know if there are concerns. The problem comes when people ignore the signs because they want to get married so badly. Then they move forward anyhow, knowing that they and their potential spouses are not equally yoked.

If you are looking for God's will regarding a mate, keep the most basic principle. Continually go back to Second Corinthians 6:14, which says, *"Do not be bound together with unbelievers; for what partnership have righteousness and lawlessness, or what fellowship has light with darkness?"* (NASB). This most basic Scripture reminds you that you simply can't make friendships, partnerships, and alliances with anyone who isn't pressed in to God and who has a different pursuit in life than you do. Mark it down: it just won't work! God's will for your mate can be largely determined by considering these things. It will aid you in deciding if the two of you together could emulate God's biblical pattern for marriage.

CLOSE YOUR EYES

Another key principle for finding God's will for the right mate is to quit looking. God brought Eve to Adam when Adam was asleep. Notice it was *God* who brought her. God didn't send Adam out looking for her! I believe this is a prophetic example of the way God intended for His people to locate their spouses. God caused Adam to be asleep when Eve arrived, not only because she was taken from His side, but also to represent that we can't go tirelessly looking for the right one. We need to let God bring them to us.

Adam wasn't running around the garden trying to locate fulfillment, even though I am sure he recognized that some form of companionship was missing. However, he kept his fellowship with God, and in turn, God saw to it that Adam's needs were met.

If you go looking here and there for a spouse, you put yourself at risk for making a mistake. Usually the fact that people go looking around at all is because they are getting antsy about waiting. This tendency can get you out of God's will in other areas too.

For example, some people will quit the church they have been part of for years because they finally decide there is no one fit to marry there. So rather than stay where God has called them to fellowship, they run to some other church they think might have some better fish in the sea! Don't allow the unsettling need to find a mate cause you to start missing God's will in multiple areas.

If you are still single, hoping to be married someday, set your standards and keep your eyes on the Lord. If God doesn't send the one for you in your time frame, remain content in Him. If it becomes increasingly difficult for you, feel confident that you can talk openly with the Lord about your feelings, just like Jesus did in the Garden of Gethsemane when He said, *"Father, if Thou be willing, remove this cup from Me..."* (Luke 22:42). He was letting the Father know how difficult His present circumstances were. However, He followed up that statement by saying, *"...nevertheless not My will, but Thine, be done"* (Luke 22:42). Share your feelings with the Lord, but then make sure you recommit your life and plans into His hands.

By keeping certain principles and standards and making a determination that you will let the Lord bring the right person for you in His time, you will not miss God's will for the right mate.

Chapter Ten

FINDING GOD'S WILL IN HEALTH, MEDICINE, AND DIVINE HEALING

He sent His word, and healed them, and delivered them from their destructions (**Psalm 107:20**).

There are two areas that every person will deal with at some point or another. They are issues pertaining to health and finances. Some Christian groups have criticized what has been labeled the "health and wealth Gospel," which basically refers to the sermons of those who preach regularly on divine healing and financial prosperity. There is some foundation to the criticism toward those who focus on little else in God's Word, such as Christian character and so forth.

However, think about this honestly: everyone deals with health and financial issues all their lives. These two areas of life affect every person alive, so we need to regularly address these subjects, not only from the practical perspective but also from the supernatural perspective. In other words, we need to teach on prudent financial management skills, but we also need to teach people the supernatural blessing of God when it comes to money. In the same way, we need to talk about a healthful diet and lifestyle, but we also need to teach God's promises concerning divine health.

We all need to be confident of God's will when it comes to our health and health-related issues, so we can make the right decisions for our lives. Some people just aren't confident of God's promises regarding divine healing, while others are struggling to follow God on making medical decisions as they work with their doctors and so forth. Let's examine some principles here that can help us locate God's will and direction for health and medicine.

GOD'S WILL FOR HEALING

Though we could write an entire book on the subject of divine healing and God's will regarding it, here we will simply establish the truth by offering a brief biblical overview. All throughout Scripture, God has always made a healing provision for His people.

When we look at the children of Israel, we always see that God made a provision for their healing. We know that when they served the Lord, healing and divine health were always theirs. In Exodus 23:25, God said to them:

> *And ye shall serve the Lord your God, and He shall bless thy bread, and thy water; and I will take sickness away from the midst of thee.*

Even when they disobeyed Him, once they called for His for help, God reached back and healed their diseases. We find His promise of healing in Psalm 103:1-3, in Psalm 107, in Jeremiah 30:17, and in so many more places in Scripture.

The icing on the cake that proves the Lord wants us healthy and well is found in the familiar passage in Isaiah 53:4-5, which tells us that Jesus was beaten with 39 lashes and shed His blood so those who call on Him can be healed. Some argue whether or not this sacrifice pertains to spiritual or physical healing, but I think the Bible clearly indicates that it is all-inclusive.

In other words, Jesus came to heal the whole person. We know this is true because Jesus provided physical healing to multitudes on the shores of Galilee just as commonly as He touched lives in other ways. He never had some hidden mystery purpose for these people to keep their diseases. When they called out to Him in faith, He healed them! In fact, we don't see anywhere in Scripture where God had some "hidden" reason as to why His people couldn't receive healing and live in divine health.

The early apostles also brought healing to the diseased. Noticeably, neither Jesus nor the apostles stopped to ask those in need of healing to wait until it was determined whether or not healing was God's will! I believe it was because these apostles knew that they were already demonstrating God's will by offering relief to people in pain. Jesus made it very clear that He came to do His Father's will, and that undoubtedly included all the healings directed toward hurting, desperate people on the shores of Galilee.

Be reassured today, if you are wondering if God wants you to be healed, He does! The "suffering" found in Scripture always relates to the suffering that comes in the form of persecution. It is the attack coming from those who hate or reject the Gospel, as we find in Second Timothy 3:12. It says, *"Yea, and all that will live godly in Christ Jesus shall suffer persecution."* This is why the apostle Paul suffered for Christ's sake. It wasn't suffering in the form of "God-designed" physical illness. That concept just doesn't stand up to the big picture of God's character in the Bible.

Realize today that no matter what illness or affliction has come your way, God wants to heal and deliver you. That is His will; you just need to believe it by faith!

DOCTORS VS. FAITH

People often ask the question, "Well, if I have faith to be healed, then is it a lack of faith to take medicine or seek the help of a doctor?" This is a valid question that has come up often throughout Christendom over the years and has raised considerable debate. Some think that if you go to the doctor you are somehow out of the will of God and God won't bless it because you need to rely solely on Him. Let's consider a few points for determining the answer to this question.

THE MEDICAL CULTURE

First, we have to understand the culture in which we live. The United States in particular is a medically dependent culture. In comparison to many other countries, we have medical intervention at our fingertips, even if we can't afford to pay for it.

Our society has created some sort of medical resource, both good and not so good, for just about everything one can dream up. So, it is understandable that many people are wary of medicine sometimes, and they want to be discerning when it comes to choosing their route for healing. In addition, Christians often want to know God's opinion on the medical remedies they choose.

We all know that although medical science has accomplished many incredible feats, it isn't without fault. Just because the doctor says something is a good idea doesn't mean it always is because some medications and procedures have a great deal of long-term side effects. So being wise in choosing certain medical interventions is fine from that perspective.

However, we have to realize that although our medically dependent culture allows some decision-making freedom regarding certain medicines and procedures, it doesn't allow for a great deal of refusal of basic medical or dental care. Most schools require immunization records. Even though there is some provision to dissent, childhood immunizations are still the expected norm. Regular eye, dental, or basic physical exams are also expected.

I have seen Christian groups from all extremes. Some are dependent on medicine for every little thing because they don't think they can expect God to heal them. Others think medical science presents far too many risks and that one should become dependent on God and faith alone for healing needs. Some go even further, saying that the addition of doctors represents a total lack of faith in God's ability to heal miraculously. Amazingly, some such people won't seek a doctor for help with an unknown disease, but they will run to the ER when they think their leg may be broken!

Here is what we have to consider, regardless of our differing beliefs: Our medically dependent society is going to expect everyone to at least receive basic medical care, such as that for physical exams, help with minor illnesses, and so forth. The medical community, and the law for that matter, aren't going to look highly on someone who refuses to take a seriously ill child to the doctor because he or she doesn't believe in using doctors.

This is especially true if something goes very wrong with the child. There have been court cases against parents who refused medical intervention for their children when they desperately needed care. In fact, special investigations are even required for anyone who doesn't actually die inside a hospital witnessed by medical staff.

The situation is different in some countries that have little to no medical resources available. People there can't always go to a doctor. We can, however, so society expects it. Therefore, we need to discern the society in which we live. Knowing all this, we need to understand that we will all be expected to seek medical help at some point if we are going to be deemed sensible and responsible individuals.

Our society has a far different expectation regarding the field of medicine than what pertains to other areas of need for which you seek help from the Lord. No one is going to question your level of responsibility or cite you for neglect because you decided to refuse the help of your local lender while praying for a financial miracle or because you wanted your complete trust for financial provision to be on God. Regardless of your financial outcome, the decision to seek the help of the bank is solely your choice. It is different with medical issues. At some point, you will be expected to seek medical care.

Now on the flip side of this, I am definitely not saying that we need to become medical and pharmaceutical junkies like many Americans have become. When we have the slightest issue, we tend to think there is some pill, herb, nutritional supplement, or potion to take for it. As much as refusing medical help can be a problem, so can an overindulgence and dependence on everything medical. Medical science has it limits and obvious shortcomings.

So does going to the doctor or taking medicine represent a certain "lack of faith"? Should an individual who obtains medical help be seen as somehow having given up on trusting God for miraculous intervention and having to settle for less?

Many refer to the Scripture about King Asa, who died because he sought the physicians over the Lord (see 2 Chron. 16:12). They think that because Asa went to the doctor that he somehow missed or displeased God. Most translations of this verse clearly indicate that Asa's condition worsened not because he went to a doctor but because he left God out of the equation altogether.

We all know that when we leave God entirely out of things and become medical junkies, we are limiting ourselves to the shortcomings of these remedies. Medical science can't solve everything, as Asa found out. We need Jesus, the Great Physician, involved in our lives, whether we go to the doctor or not.

I don't believe God looks at something like seeking medical help as the primary indicator to determine whether we have a lack of faith. I don't think God looks as much at that as He looks at what our faith supply was long before the illness ever came along! He knows how much or little spiritual time we invested or perhaps how mature we were in certain areas of faith well before we made the appointment with the doctor.

Also, God understands the society we live in and knows we will be expected to receive some measure of medical help for numerous things.

Realize that when it comes to faith, some people are able to trust God for certain issues and will see instant results. Yet, in other areas, they still need to develop their faith and give it time to grow. Where King Asa made his mistake was that he quit looking to the Lord as his ultimate source and placed his trust in physicians far above God. Calling the doctor or seeking help from medicine was not the deciding factor on Asa's faith or lack thereof, nor will it be for us.

If you are actively pursuing the Lord and you find the need to get medical help, don't feel like the Lord is somehow offended at your faith skills. Let the situation serve to show you that perhaps you need to grow your faith or ability to receive healing in that area, either for the first time or as a refresher course. Use it as an opportunity to build yourself up on God's promises regarding healing. Yet, again, the best time to build your faith in general is not when the storm is upon you but rather before the storm comes.

KNOW YOUR FAITH LEVEL

Some people want to jump out in faith for healing on something, but faith isn't automatic. Of course, you can experience the "gift of faith" found in First Corinthians 12:9, which is a momentary surge of supernatural faith that comes from the Holy Spirit. This gift is a supernatural faith that you didn't have to develop. It just comes upon you for a particular situation.

However, most of the faith needed for getting our prayers answered and so forth must be developed by reading and meditating in God's Word (see Rom. 10:17) coupled with prayer (see Jude 1:20; Matt. 17:21). We all need to grow in this type of faith because the Bible tells us this is how a Christian must live. Four times the Bible says, *"The just shall live by faith"* (see Hab. 2:4; Rom. 1:17; Gal. 3:11; Heb. 10:38). As it's repeated four times, this must be a pretty important ingredient to having success in our spiritual walk with God.

All throughout the ministry of both Jesus and the early apostles, people were healed specifically because of their faith to receive the healing. Among countless other similar examples, we see how Jesus looked for faith when the blind men came to Him for healing in Matthew 9:27-30. Jesus asked them, *"… Believe ye that I am able to do this?"* (Matt. 9:28). Once Jesus felt confident their faith was able, the blind were healed. Then in Acts 14:8-10, Paul ministered to a crippled man at Lystra. The Bible says that Paul looked at him, *"…perceiving that he had faith to be healed"* (Acts 14:9).

The Bible shows convincing evidence that if we want to be healed by God, it is going to require faith, and we know that the Bible teaches us that faith is developed through a process and is something we all have to grow in. A good example is with Peter; Jesus prayed for him during a time of testing right before the crucifixion. He said:

...Simon, Simon, behold, Satan hath desired to have you, that he may sift you as wheat; but I have prayed for thee, that thy faith fail not... (Luke 22:31-32).

In other words, Jesus was telling Peter that His specific prayer was that Peter's level of faith would be able to withstand what he was about to walk through. This is probably because Jesus already knew that Peter's faith level was shaky at that time.

We need to determine our own faith levels for certain things that we face too. Some things we are ready to war against, while other things require us to get back into our Bibles and prayer closets and build some faith muscles.

We find a very different Peter after Pentecost, when instead of cowering at the challenge at hand, he confronted those who crucified Jesus in his very first recorded sermon (see Acts 2). We can see that Peter had progressed in his faith and was ready to confront the very thing that intimidated him previously. This time he overcame it!

As you face certain battles against sickness and wrestle with whether you should include the help of a doctor, know what your faith level is going into the situation. If your heart is fearful and you're second guessing yourself, by all means call the doctor! Then afterward, get in your prayer closet so that you can allow the Holy Spirit to rise up inside you to defeat whatever the illness might be. We all have areas in which we either need to develop faith or refresh it.

You can know a lot about your faith level based on how much time you spend feeding on spiritual things, particularly surrounding your situation. The more habitual you are about meditating in God's Word and praying, the more skillful you will become, and it will make your level of faith stronger.

In addition to that, we all need teachers and spiritual leaders whom we can hear preach on subjects such as divine healing. This also causes us to become more knowledgeable in the Scriptures so we can learn how to use these truths from God's Word like a weapon of war (see Eph. 6:17; Heb. 4:12).

If you have made the habit of doing the things necessary to develop your faith for healing before the attack of infirmity comes, you will naturally be more confident of the victory. You will know your faith level, and it will help you respond accordingly. If your faith level is low because you know you haven't developed in that area, then begin now! Don't just give up on divine healing through faith after you get home from the doctor's office knowing you haven't received a good diagnosis. Start increasing your faith level!

I like the story about one man that I read in a Christian newsletter years ago. The man became ill with a serious heart problem. He was so weak and tired that he could barely do anything at all. Because he felt so badly and needed some relief, he went to the doctor. The doctors said his heart was barely functioning and that he needed a transplant. He had never even been previously diagnosed with any form of heart disease.

He just told the doctor, "Doctor, you just give me your recommended medicine to get me feeling at least a little better, and I am going to go home and get with God for my healing!" The man didn't resist the medicine and followed all the instructions of his doctor. He even let them put him on the heart transplant list.

But in the meantime, he began increasing his faith level in order to get a miracle. He stayed in the Bible and quoted Scriptures on healing out loud. He built expectancy in himself every day through God's Word and in prayer. One day he even decided to mow the lawn as a confident step of faith. He could only do a few steps, but he was determined he wouldn't take no for an answer and wanted to step out in faith.

To make a long story short, in less than two years, doctors found that he didn't need the heart transplant after all, and in fact, they told him that tests showed amazing results. It was as if he had a brand-new heart! He was completely healed!

What we can learn from this is that when the man first got the diagnosis, he went home and assessed his faith level and did what was needed to build it up to the level necessary. By doing so, he came out in victory. This is God's will for you also, to rise up in victory over all sickness and infirmity.

So don't feel like you should or shouldn't go to the doctor. Our society expects you to receive certain medical care for numerous things, so you can't just take the stance of having no medical intervention in the name of faith and prayer. However, you need to also build your faith so that ultimately your trust is in the Living God and not in what medical science can provide. If you have that priority straight, you will stay in God's will for your healing. This will also help you effectively decide how to incorporate the dimension of medicine when necessary.

TAKING MEDICATION

During the process of trusting God for healing, people often ask if or how long they should continue taking prescription or even over-the-counter medicines. Some people have been prescribed lifelong medicines, such as insulin, high blood pressure or heart medicines, and so forth. To quit taking them in the name of faith could prove detrimental if the person's faith isn't up to the task or simply because the process of stopping certain medicines needs to be done under the guidance of a medical professional.

It is understandable that most people who have been on medicines long term want nothing more than to be healed and to be done taking them. Therefore, they commonly want to know what is an acceptable approach to finally placing all their dependence on faith and ultimately ending their dependence on these medicines.

The truth is that we don't want to step out on assumed faith but rather on true faith that is evidenced by tangible results. If people aren't seeing tangible results in their bodies just yet, then I like to suggest that they do three things while they continue to take their medicine:

1. *Take the medicine of God's Word along with your natural medicine.* Each time you take your medicine, read a Scripture out loud and declare that God's Word and promises are working like medicine in your body (see Prov. 4:20-22). Keep building your faith this way and allow the medicine of

God's Word to in effect "overtake you" until healing is complete. If you take the medicine of God's Word every day in this manner, it will supernaturally work inside you. In addition, declare that the natural medicine you are taking will work with your body and not against it, and that you will not suffer any ill effects while taking it.

I personally know many people who have done this and are medicine-free today.

2. *Look for the natural manifestations of healing.* As God's healing medicine begins to work in you, the evidence will begin to manifest itself in an obvious way. This is often through a decreased dependence on natural medicine. Perhaps your natural medicine will need to be reduced or your body will begin to reject the need for the natural medicine. Therefore, continue to take your medicine and allow your body to reduce its need as healing begins to manifest. Your doctor should obviously be able to confirm this is the case.

3. *Let your doctor be a part of the decision on stopping or changing your medicine.* This doesn't necessarily mean that a doctor should have the final say on all your medical decisions, but you should consider his or her professional input on your medical condition and the best time and method to stop taking a certain medicine. Though the final say is your own, and the limited ability of natural

medicine needs to be kept in mind, the process of stopping certain medicines without medical oversight can impose adverse effects. This is why it is important to discuss medicinal changes with a medical professional.

Along with this advice, allow the Holy Spirit to drop wisdom into your heart. As you consider natural medicine in light of these points, let God speak to your spirit and follow the sound of His voice. The Lord inside you will not let you fail. Even if you take natural medicine, it's important to never forget that medical science can only answer a limited number of problems. Therefore, do what is necessary spiritually to shift your predominant trust in medicine over to God and His promises. We always have to remind ourselves that God's healing power supersedes all natural remedies and we need to build our faith in that every day.

HEARING GOD FOR MEDICAL DECISIONS

Everyone needs to make decisions as to what medical intervention is right for them. From over-the-counter meds on up to the more involved medical procedures, some thought is often required as to which medical choices are the best for you or your family. Some people have to make medical decisions with a doctor when a loved one is critically ill and the medical staff is asking the family to give consent for certain things. Although there isn't always an easy, cut-and-dried answer for some of these decisions, following the basic principles for finding God's

will that we have learned thus far, in addition to some key principles, will help.

TRUSTED RESOURCES

The issue of major medical decisions is one area in which
I believe it pays to obtain the input of those in your life who
have a proven track record of walking out the will of God in
their own lives. When you are faced with making a challenging medical decision, your pastor, spiritual church leaders, and
mature Christian friends can offer wise counsel. These mature
saints can often speak from experience because they have fruit
from times in their own lives when they launched out with God
and their steps of faith proved to be right.

Sometimes when people get into situations where they are
presented with a medical decision that needs to be answered
right now, they often let go of trusted resources. Stay with those
things that you have trusted and proven in the past, and don't
react outside of your trusted norm just because doctors and relatives are demanding an answer.

RESPECT THE DOCTOR AS
A PROFESSIONAL

I have seen many well-meaning Christian people almost dis-
respect doctors' opinions and advice simply because they know
that the doctor doesn't understand or agree with God's healing
power. In the name of healing and God's Word, they treat
doctors almost like they don't know anything. I have watched

well-meaning Christians treat doctors as if their medical diagnoses are ludicrous. At the same time, I also realize that some doctors are ignorant concerning the miraculous power of our God.

When your loved one is in need of medical care and you are there interacting with the medical staff, you need the doctors on your side, and you need to work with them. As Christians, we obviously know inside information about Jesus' healing power, but we need to use wisdom in how it is presented. We need wisdom in how we present the Gospel to people in general. Sure, there are times when doctors may try to advise us in direct opposition to God, but we must handle them tastefully even when we disagree with them.

Many years ago, when my father nearly died in a medical coma from an infection, my family and I had to work with medical staff every day. We respected what they wanted and talked professionally with them about certain suggestions (and sometimes even demands) that they had. We knew in the end they wanted to do what was best for our dad, and we couldn't speak to them like religious fanatics. At the same time, we knew the devil was using their negative medical conclusions to discourage our faith at times. Though spoken with good intentions from their educational perspective, we knew there was an unseen war in the spirit realm behind those words. Yet, we still had to continue to work alongside them and also be able to tactfully dismiss from our minds their beliefs that our dad might not recover.

On one occasion, nearing the time when my dad rose up from what was thought to be his deathbed, the doctors wanted to insert a tracheotomy into his throat. We were standing on every thread of faith for his recovery. In that effort, my sister said, "Doctor, is there any way we can wait another day? If he doesn't improve the way you want, we are fine with what you want to do." We were asking for more time, expecting God to intervene.

Do you know what happened? He improved, and the doctors never did the tracheotomy! We worked with the doctors and made them feel that we appreciated their professional wisdom and insight, while at the same time we kept our faith. When our faith disagreed with what the doctors wanted, we talked things over with them and reaffirmed that we were just trying to make wise choices while we thought over their advice.

LISTEN TO YOUR SPIRIT

Lastly, as you make medical decisions, go back to the principle of listening to God in your spirit. I believe this is one environment in which God's voice inside you becomes the loudest. Sometimes, it's that wary feeling. You don't have to be concerned that your reservations are some odd form of "doctor-phobia" when you know that you are supportive of the doctor. Instead, something down inside you just doesn't feel right about a certain medical procedure the medical team is recommending. You don't have to present it to them in the form of "God told me not to do it!" If your spirit is reserved on it, then perhaps just ask them if it's feasible to wait a day or two. Rest assured the Holy Spirit will speak into your heart so you can make the right decisions.

God wants you well. For every person, there is a different road to walk out God's divine will for healing. God isn't offended by doctors if you trust Him first and foremost and build your faith in that fact. What God really wants is for you to trust Him as you walk the road to divine health.

I have no doubt that the more we do this, the more we will live free of illness and disease. We will see more instantaneous divine healings and miracles too!

God's will for you is healing, and if you know that, you don't need to worry about how He walks you through it!

Chapter Eleven

FINDING GOD'S WILL FOR CHOOSING A CHURCH

Not forsaking the assembling of ourselves together, as the manner of some is; but exhorting one another: and so much the more, as ye see the day approaching (**Hebrews 10:25**).

I have said it many times throughout my life—one of the safest places to be during the dangerous last days that the Bible talks about is in a good local church. A local church has such a strong ability to keep Christians grounded and growing properly in their spiritual walk.

Often those who become disillusioned with church and quit going for whatever reason tend to take on an unbalanced spiritual approach to things. Even if their reason for not going to church was because the church didn't handle them right or they felt hurt by it, they still tend to lose a certain needed balance in spiritual things.

When we don't continually rub shoulders with other believers who are each a little bit different than we are, we never have to adapt our Christian experience to anyone but ourselves. When that happens, our doctrine is never countered by anyone else. We can't learn how to work with others in a spiritual environment. We also miss learning the valuable lesson of being submitted to the church structure. Without it, the risk is that we begin to think that everything we are doing is right in our own eyes. We never hear any good preaching to help us cross-examine our own hearts.

Also if we don't attend church, our lives are not being regularly impacted by the corporate anointing. There is something special about the corporate anointing. It changes our entire outlook as it washes over us during worship or times of special ministry. Many Christians who leave off getting connected to a good church seem to lose a certain right balance in their approach to spiritual things because they never experience the corporate anointing.

As we look at the New Testament, we see that the early believers made assembling together a priority. There are many arguments about how the modern-day example of organized church didn't exist at that time. Some attempt to use this to prove that the current model of church is somehow not biblically accurate and that home groups are more appropriate.

However, we see that these early believers went to church. In fact, Acts 2:46 says they assembled both in the temple and in homes. Knowing this, it only stands to reason that when 3000 and then 5000 were added to the Church shortly after Pentecost, these new Christians had times of corporate assembly. I believe they realized how much they needed those gathering times in order to face life every day.

Most of us know Hebrews 10:25, which says:

Not forsaking the assembling of ourselves together, as the manner of some is; but exhorting one another: and so much the more, as ye see the day approaching.

Notice that it says *"as the manner of some is."* Some translations say, *"as is the habit of some"* (NASB). Even back then, people had excuses for why they didn't think they needed to assemble or go to church with other Christians. This Scripture tells us that not only do we need to assemble, but we need it even more as the end of the age approaches.

There is no doubt that it is God's will for each of us to find a good church where we can be fed and experience healthy Christian growth in our lives. Of course, I realize that not everyone lives in a geographical location where a good church exists or where church options abound, but that doesn't negate the fact that we need other believers if we want to grow. Assembling with other believers is one of the needed ingredients to a healthy spiritual diet. Without it our growth will become stunted.

In this chapter, I will cover a few brief principles to help you locate a good church and also know how to listen to God about what church He wants you to attend. Not only do you need a church, but you need to go where God wants you.

In addition, I will discuss how to switch from one church to another. I think people need to find a church and, once they do, make a point of putting their roots down for the long haul. Church isn't like choosing a restaurant or a bank. I once heard a man say, "Church isn't just a teaching or worship center; it's a family." That is so true. I am amazed at how those who attend the same church develop a special camaraderie.

In a healthy church the people take care of one another just like a family does. That is why when people leave a church, there is often a sense of loss or the feeling like a family member has left that special bond of fellowship unique to the family. It isn't like changing to a new bank. A spiritual bond goes with church involvement. However, certain occasions can make it necessary for a person to switch to a different church, but there is a proper way in the scope of God's will to go about it.

WHAT MAKES A GOOD CHURCH

There is no perfect church. Put two human beings in any room, and we're asking for trouble! There will be differences of opinions, ideas, and values. No pastor is perfect, but then neither are there any perfect sheep. So we have to realize that no matter what church we choose, there will be flaws, and there will be things that deviate from our personal preferences. We must remind ourselves of this key factor. The reason many people get out of God's will regarding a church is because they are looking for some kind of perfect utopia. They come to a church wanting to make sure it meets all the criteria on their list.

When we first started our church, a family visited, and we shook their hands after the service. Our children's ministry back then was still pretty small, and most of the kids were combined into one group, except for the very youngest children. Actually, we only had two rooms for the kids at that time: the tiny nursery room and then one larger room for all the others.

We asked this couple if they enjoyed the service and so forth. The wife responded, saying, "We liked it a lot, but we are looking for a church where all the kids are in separate classrooms by their age." She wanted it to be like school. She knew the church was just starting, but this was her criteria, among other things, and because of it, they didn't stay.

Every church has had people visit who thought the church didn't have available all the things important to them. However, we must realize that no church is able to be all things to all people, so we can't determine if a church is a good one based on whether or not it meets all our personal preferences; we can't rule it out just because it has a few flaws.

As you pray about God's will for you in finding a church, you need to locate a quality church. There are key characteristics that constitute a good church. These are not so much preferences but rather the framework that will ultimately make the church strong no matter how new or old, large or small. The church may only have a fledgling children's ministry, but if the framework is in place, you are looking at a good church.

PREACHING OF THE WORD

This is probably the number one characteristic, and it will spill over into all areas of the church. The pastor should lead the way and make sure that the messages and the various avenues of ministry are providing sound Bible feeding. Now when I say sound Bible feeding and preaching of the Word, I mean sermons that teach and mature people in the Scriptures, not messages that just tickle their ears or engage their interest.

Some preachers are great orators, but they don't feed the sheep true spiritual food. There is little Word going forth, even though many good things are said. If you are in a good church, you should begin to gain biblical knowledge. The preaching should not only get you excited but should challenge you to change and grow. It will make you stronger.

Again, although none of us has the perfect Bible knowledge on every subject, the doctrine of the church should be sound overall. That doesn't mean the church won't have to walk through some of the pastor's own developing knowledge in certain things from Scripture, but as the pastor preaches, the doctrinal foundation should be sound. I preached some things years ago that I felt so strongly about at the time, but now I look back and see how I needed to tweak what was presented. Though I had areas that needed to mature, my doctrinal foundation has always remained constant.

HOLY SPIRIT WELCOMED

In a good church, the Holy Spirit is given liberty. Every church may have a different way of facilitating it, but the gifts of the Spirit should be in manifestation on a regular basis. I don't believe this just needs to be in the main services but also among the discipleship groups, children's ministry, and other areas of ministry the church may have available.

The key is that those who attend need to accept and be willing to flow in line with how that particular church incorporates the anointing. One church may do so one way, while the church down the street may do it differently.

For example, we love prophecy in our church. In fact, we train people in prophecy during their discipleship groups so they can develop themselves in the prophetic and be used in the various venues God may open for them. However, we typically limit the opportunity to prophesy to those who have earned trust among the sheep and to those who are involved in discipleship.

Additionally, we typically don't let congregational members interrupt a service to give a word of prophecy, unless we open the floor for such, and even then, we normally open that only to trusted vessels. Most of the ministry in a main service will come from the pastors.

Other churches may allow prophecy to flow differently and have different protocol for such things, but the key is that the Holy Spirit is allowed to flow and there is a place to receive Spirit-filled ministry.

I am not trying to say one method is more right than another per se, but rather that whatever church you go to, you need to adapt to that church's protocol. What you are really looking for, in the end, is that there is a place made for the gifts of the Spirit to manifest and for the anointing to flow.

AN ENVIRONMENT OF EXCELLENCE

Many churches today lack a certain quality of order and excellence. They don't start services on time, the service structure is haphazard, and order is lacking among those serving. In some churches, you can't tell who the ushers are, the children's classrooms are a mess, and the interior finishes need work. Some rooms are cluttered, ceiling tiles are stained and falling, floor boards are broken, and there is an overall lack of order. I have even been in churches where the bathrooms barely work! This lack of excellence in the facility itself might be more forgivable in some poorer countries, but for the most part in the United States this can be avoided and doesn't represent the ministry well.

When the surroundings and service order are shoddy, it says something about how the church is being operated behind the scenes. This tendency toward a lack of order is more common among Charismatic churches, and it gives Spirit-filled circles a bad name. It just misrepresents God's Kingdom in general.

I understand creating excellence is a process. I know if a church takes over an older building, it takes time to fix up every nook and cranny. However, it becomes an issue when the areas that are supposed to be "fixed up" still look unkempt. I truly believe an outward lack of excellence is a visible sign of an internal lack of excellence.

When you walk into a good church, greeters, ushers, children's workers, quality print material, and clean surroundings should be the first things that greet you. Even in the smallest of churches, the environment should be sharp and well manicured, and the general schedule of things should be operated with order.

A CULTURE OF INTEGRITY

A culture of integrity includes several things. Not only should the pastor and leadership team work hard to represent integrity as they run the ministry, but they should exhibit integrity in their personal lives as well. A culture of integrity also means that the pastor isn't afraid to expect a holy standard among the people. Some pastors today don't preach the commands of Scripture; they make everything sound like optional suggestions, as if people's standard for living can be whatever they deem appropriate.

If a church carries integrity it will be evident in the atmosphere. You will be able to discern from the pastor that he or she works hard to live a clean life and that he makes sure that God's church is operated in an ethical and biblical manner.

MINISTRY CONSTANTLY DEVELOPS

Lastly, one of the key signs of a good church is that ministries for people from all walks of life are developed. Of course, depending on the church's size, it may not include everything one would want for ministry, but a good church will progress because it keeps in mind the needs of people. The level of ministry our church has available today is far beyond what it was ten years ago! Ten years from now, there will be countless more arms of ministry to meet people's needs. The key is that if the ministry is a quality one, it will show progression.

This doesn't necessarily mean that the church will double in numbers. Truthfully, in some geographical locations that is difficult. Some churches in remote locations or small farm communities just don't have the numbers in terms of people to always draw from. A better sign of progression is that the ministry is constantly developing so that it can be more effective for those who attend and serve and also for those in the community. A good church will continually make changes so it can be sure people's needs are being met. It will eliminate things that have become outdated in order to make way for fresh, innovative ministry.

An example of this is seen in Acts 6, when the apostles had to appoint helpers to meet the needs of the widows. The church progressed in order to provide better ministry to those in need.

Once you establish that the church you are considering is a good one, you can more clearly listen to whether or not God has called you to attend there.

WHEN OPTIONS ARE LIMITED

Not every locale has the ideal church; in fact, some communities don't even have a Spirit-filled church. So what do you do in order to stay in God's will for going to church if a good one isn't available where you live?

First of all, realize that God understands this dilemma that many people feel. I personally would move to where there was a good church; however, I know for countless reasons, this isn't possible for everyone. Some people are disabled and can't even leave the house to go to church. Some manage family farms; others are teens who live with their parents, and so forth. This special group is not the majority. However, if you are in the category where you just don't feel there is a good church in your area and you can't move to where one is located, I would consider the following:

1. *Consider the best option available.* Perhaps there is a mainline church you can go to that will at least give you a sense of belonging with those who

maintain Christian beliefs. Just having a place to go is helpful. Perhaps there are a few options, even Spirit-filled ones, but none seem to fulfill what you were hoping for. In that case, realize that God knows this, and He can help you flourish even in a less-than-ideal setting.

However, if your church isn't what you are hungry for, you *can't* expect to be the factor that brings reform to that church someday. God doesn't appoint members of the congregation to somehow enlighten the pastor. Sure, sheep can interact with the pastor, and we can all grow by interacting with each other, but there isn't any "calling" that you can have to bring radical change to a church. No matter what church you attend, you need to be submitted to the way that church is run.

2. *Connect with ministries via other means.* There are countless ministries on television, online, and at conferences that you can connect with or go to their meetings and so forth. Consider signing up for their newsletters. Participating in such a ministry will also give you a sense of belonging with those who share your same spiritual vision and offer some rich feeding that you need. As a teenager, I lived in a small town that didn't have many church options, but I got on the mailing lists of many powerful ministries worldwide, and these helped me grow to where I am today.

3. *Consider making a special sacrifice.* Perhaps consider, if you are able, driving a longer-than-usual distance to a nearby larger community to attend church. One couple who has been in our church since we started drives into town from a farm community that is close to 100 miles away. They come almost every Sunday morning, weather permitting, and have done so for 14 years. They just decided that it pays to put in the distance to attend a quality church. We have several others who drive close to 50 miles to come to church as well.

WHAT CHURCH HAS GOD CALLED ME TO?

When multiple church options are available in your community, the next step is knowing how to find God's will for the right church. First, you must determine if the one you are considering meets the basic criteria for a good church. Second, you must remind yourself that no church is perfect, nor are you perfect, so there is no flawless church experience.

Once you have established these two factors, which many people fail to do repeatedly, then you need to ask the Lord where He has called you. Understand that God will call you where He knows you will bloom effectively and also grow the most spiritually. The Lord knows what you need! Church should not only encourage and uplift you, but it should sometimes get in your space cushion and challenge you.

Once you've established the church you are considering is a good church, knowing that no church is perfect, begin to put into practice the principles in this book for locating the will of God. Once you do so, here are a couple of key ingredients for deciding on your church. If you keep them in the forefront of your thinking, you will feel more settled and won't be as apt to uproot yourself when those imperfect church experiences arise.

The two ingredients are: (1) the church should cause you to bloom, and (2) the church should cause you to be challenged. The reason these are so important is that they are the two key ingredients the Holy Spirit wants for your life so you can grow. He wants you to flourish so you can be used by Him for a good purpose, and He also wants to challenge you in your weaknesses. Ask yourself:

CAN I BLOOM IN THIS CHURCH?

Everyone has varying gifts and talents. Some churches are more conducive to certain gifts over others. Of course, your church may not have in place everything it will eventually one day, but you must still look at the ways you feel you can bloom in that church. Your first indication may just be that you feel connected to the warm, friendly atmosphere of the people there. That is a good indicator that you can bloom there because you feel loved.

Perhaps you are hungry to learn more about the gifts of the Spirit, and you know this church focuses a lot on them. Then you can be confident that as you come into that environment, you will begin to flourish. You can bloom or flourish both directly and indirectly. Directly will be through the areas you are able to get involved in as the church makes them available to you. Indirectly will be what you receive just by being a part of it.

HOW COULD I GROW IN THIS CHURCH?

If you need to grow in the area of financial excellence, and you know that is something the pastor preaches and covers in his messages, it's possible the church will be a good resource to help you in that area. If you know you have a habit of getting too busy outside of spiritual things with your schedule, maybe a church with lots of activities and areas to serve in is just what you need to keep you going in the right direction. If you have some sin habits, look for a church that you know will preach righteous living and keep you accountable. If you tend to be overcome easily by depression and emotion, maybe you need a church that presses you to rise above that behavior.

When you choose a church because you want it to challenge your weak areas and you know it has what's best for you, you will be apt to stick it out even when you have a "fleshly season" in your spiritual walk. You won't be as apt to move on to some other church just because you feel challenged to grow.

If you consider the things I have discussed thus far, you will be well on your way to finding God's will for you concerning a church. Once you do, put your roots in and stay with it. Most lasting growth that comes from attending a church doesn't come in just a few short months. The ones who go furthest are those who can stay with it for the long term and truly get the DNA of their church environment.

PROPER REASONS TO CHOOSE A NEW CHURCH

People always ask the question, "Is it ever God's will for me to leave a church and go on to new one?" Yes, there are the proper reasons for changing churches, and we need to discuss them briefly. There is so much debate and hurt feelings over this subject, but valid reasons do exist for leaving a current church and going to a new one. Sometimes problems arise because people leave for wrong reasons, or sometimes they leave with the wrong methods. Other times the pastors use wrong methods in responding to people who leave.

The key is that we want to be biblical in how we handle God's beloved churches so we can stay in the will of God. Consider two factors that are indicators that it is time to move on to a different church:

DIFFERENT FLAVORS

Churches are like ice cream. They come in different flavors, but they are all still ice cream. Even if you have been in a church for some time, you may find that your church's expressions and directions can change. Some churches that started out as good churches lose the qualities of a good church. In some cases, a new pastor comes in, and the vision and the direction of the church changes. Your own spiritual growth may develop differently than the church you have been in, and you stop flourishing there.

In some cases, people are only in a certain church because a church more in line with their preferences wasn't available at the time. Then one across town opens, and they feel like they want to be a part of it. I don't think the Holy Spirit is bothered by these reasons for changing churches. He wants us fulfilled in our church experience overall.

Changing churches because of differences in flavor is an acceptable reason, assuming that your flavor isn't a fleshly one. Some people just want to go back to dead religion as their "flavor" because they don't want their flesh to be in contrast with the Spirit-filled anointing in a church. They want a "flavor" that feeds their flesh. Some want a new "flavor" because they have hidden sin and don't want the people in their current church who know them to figure it out. Sometimes people want a new church so they can hide something or run from their pastor's correction. However, changing because of preferences over different expressions in and of itself is fine.

HEART CHANGE

This one isn't always a good reason to leave, but it is a necessary one: when your heart is no longer feeling connected to a church, then it's probably time to move on. If you don't, your heart will possibly become offended, and that's when you can get into fault finding and criticism. Those things are *never* the will of God. If your heart has changed toward your church, and you put up mental walls every time you attend, do yourself a favor and make plans to relocate.

The key is, don't let your heart become offended, and don't make the decision because you listened to someone else bad-mouth the ministry. Make the decision for yourself and by yourself without the input of other discontented sheep. My advice is never leave with a group that decides to all leave together. Even if you feel you must leave because the church or pastor has fallen into gross sin or false doctrine, keep to yourself.

Regardless of your reason for leaving, right or wrong, after you leave, it's best to stay disconnected from others who left. You don't want the reasons you left to put you into gossip and cause you to get out of God's will by talking badly. You just don't want to displease the Lord by spreading negative things about fellow believers, pastors, or churches.

MOVE OR JOB CHANGE

Some people simply change churches because of a job transfer. Again, I would move to a new place based on the church there, but not everyone's occupation gives them that choice. Obviously, changing churches due to a move is acceptable and understandable.

ONE THING THAT IS NEVER GOD'S WILL

One thing that is *never* God's will when it comes to church transference is strife, division, gossip, or organized group efforts to hurt a church. It is amazing how many people think nothing about hurling out hate toward churches.

Each of us needs to be reminded of the biblical requirement of love and the commandment to not spread gossip against one another. The Bible is clear that we cannot be hateful and unkind toward our fellow brothers and sisters and be considered a friend of God (see 1 John 2:9-11; 4:8,20).

In fact, the Bible says that this behavior will blind us. Look at First John 2:11, which says:

> *But he that hateth his brother is in darkness, and walketh in darkness, and knoweth not whither he goeth, because that darkness hath blinded his eyes.*

This is why we don't want to get involved in strife and division with any member of the Body of Christ. It will blind us, and we will miss God's will for our lives!

However, Christians do this all the time with each other and with churches and think nothing of it, and they believe God won't notice. I think many people are walking around in the dark and don't even realize it. They don't know they are out of God's will.

No matter what your church experience was or why you left your church, don't get out of God's will because you can't stop being offended. Don't keep the secret hope in your heart that your previous church will begin to suffer one day. Avoid connecting with others who left because somehow you want to feel better about your situation.

If you have taken part in anything against a church that promotes division, even if that church or pastor was clearly in the wrong, repent and stay in God's will for love and unity in the Body of Christ. It will keep you in the will of God.

God wants you to find His will for a good church; the key is keeping your heart motives pure and allowing God to change you. As you walk your spiritual journey, know that church, even with its faults, will be the safest place and a primary ingredient to keeping you in the will of God.

Chapter Twelve

WHEN GOD'S WILL MATCHES YOUR HEART'S DESIRE

If ye abide in Me, and My words abide in you, ye shall ask what ye will, and it shall be done unto you (**John 15:7**).

As we have reviewed many principles for hearing and following the will of God for our lives, we need to cover one key point about God's character when it comes to His divine will. Before we do, let's briefly review some of the key principles for locating the will of God that we have discussed throughout this book.

1. *Never forget that you can know God's will.* Remember God isn't trying to hide His will from you. He is making it available to you.

2. *Listen to God from within you.* The Holy Spirit lives inside you, and He wants to communicate with you directly. Learn to listen to your own spirit before you listen to everything else.

3. *Always go back to the Bible.* Look up Scriptures that pertain to the area you are listening to God about. Let the Word speak.

4. *Listen to others.* God uses prophets and trusted people to speak into your life. You just need to seek the right ones with a pure heart motive so you can stay on track.

5. *Be wise with circumstances.* Occasionally, although this is not His primary form of communication, God will use circumstances to speak to you. You just have to know how to discern which things God is using to speak.

6. *Narrow down the input.* Sometimes if you listen to too many things and too many people, you get confused. Narrow down the playing field to your most trusted resources.

7. *Calm down and listen.* It's always more challenging to hear God in the midst of a crises and chaos when you are worked up. When you settle down, you are more apt to hear the Lord.

As you adopt these principles, you will learn to hear God and follow God's will like you have always wanted to do. Yet, as you grow with God, you need to realize that your relationship to the Lord is a mutual one. In other words, God is also interested in *your will*. You might be saying, "Did I hear you correctly? You mean God cares about the things I want?" Yes!

Think about it for a moment. In a marriage, the likes, dislikes, and interests of both partners come into play. That is what relationship is all about.

I understand that relationship is different with the Lord because He is all wise. You need to do things His way because He is smarter than you are, and He always knows what He is doing. By making a firm commitment to follow and obey Him, you will live a safer and more fulfilled life. At the same time, what few are willing to consider is that God cares about the things that are important to you when those things don't violate His Word.

For example, the Lord knows that having a clean, well-manicured home is important to me. It always has been. My mother was an incredible homemaker, and her house was never dirty, so that is how I grew up.

When my husband and I got married, it was the first time I had lived away from home. We lived for a short time in a nice two-bedroom apartment, but my husband wanted us to get a house. We began looking, but the houses in our budget range—well, let's just say they were less than desirable. OK, I will say it: they were awful!

We toured countless homes with stained carpets, beat up finishes, and ghastly décor. After looking at them, I told him that I didn't want to buy a house anymore! Today we know a few more things about renovation than we did back then, but we are not handy people when it comes to fixing up a house. We can barely hang a towel rack! Plus, we were very young and had never owned a home, so we needed it to be move-in ready.

Now, I suppose some people would have moved into some of the homes we looked at, but I just couldn't. They felt icky and stinky. I just said, "Lord I know we can't afford a better one, but I don't want a house if this is what I have to live in."

Do you know what God did? He showed us a house next to the home of my parents, with whom we have a great relationship. It had come on the market, and my husband was determined to look at it. I thought, There is no way we can afford it. It was several thousand dollars above our budget, so I thought, No way. We looked at it, however, and I loved it! It was tiny, but it was a perfectly clean little dollhouse.

To make a long story short, several unusual things fell into place, we bought the house, and it never once strained our budget. It was truly a miracle! I realized from this that God cares about what is important to us! God gave me a cute, clean house. He has always done the same for us year after year because He knows this area is important to me.

Now I didn't go overboard on my house wants, but God knew there was a house out there that I would feel comfortable living in, and He met the desires of my heart. He went above and beyond what I thought would be possible at that time.

God cares about what is important to you as well. Realize that God loves your uniqueness and is interested in the things you like as long as those interests line up with the ways of God. So how can you be sure? There are several key signs.

YOU ARE COMMITTED

If you want to be confident that God is going to get involved and give you the desires of your heart, you need to assure yourself of one key thing. Psalm 37:4-5 says:

Delight thyself also in the Lord; and He shall give thee the desires of thine heart. Commit thy way unto the Lord; trust also in Him; and He shall bring it to pass.

We can see from these familiar verses that we get the desires of our hearts because we are committed to the Lord. I like to say it this way: if we commit to God, He will commit to us. I learned that God became defensive of what was important to me because He knew I defended what was important to Him. He took something simple like a desire for a decent and clean house and granted it.

You see, many Christians never feel confident that God gets involved or notices the desires of their hearts. It's not that He doesn't but rather perhaps that they don't see it because they are too busy focusing on themselves and not making sure that they are considering what is important to the Lord every day.

Not too long ago, my husband and I were laughing with our kids and making funny jokes with each other all evening. We are a family that loves to tease and laugh. Gradually, we all began to settle down for the night, still teasing and running into each other's bedrooms here and there.

As my husband and I were getting ready to retire, suddenly I felt the Lord was enjoying the family time almost as if He wanted to participate in the fun. Now this may sound silly, but it was as if I heard the Lord say, "Can I laugh with you too?" I felt badly that I never thought to include the Lord in the fun. I reminded myself that God loves our fellowship and wants to have fun with us. He wants to participate in even the funny things of our lives.

I began to wonder how many things we deal with every day that we inadvertently leave God out of. I believe God wants our commitment because He is so deeply committed to us. He wants the relationship to be mutual to the point that we think simultaneously with Him and we don't consider anything without His involvement.

When we are committed to the Lord this way, we don't have to feel like getting answers to prayer or staying in His will are a challenge. This is because a developed relationship gives us a certain measure of confidence. If our way is committed to Him, we know He will bring the desires we have into manifestation.

YOUR DESIRES EMULATE HIS WORD

Many of us quote a powerful Scripture, and have perhaps even memorized it, about knowing God's will when we pray for certain things.

> *And this is the confidence that we have in Him, that,*
> *if we ask any thing according to His will, He heareth*
> *us: and if we know that He hear us, whatsoever we*
> *ask, we know that we have the petitions that we*
> *desired of Him* (1 John 5:14-15).

From these verses, we know that we need to ask things that are in line with His will. If we want God to answer our prayers or give us the desires of our hearts, we need to make certain that we are lined up with His will.

The first question most people ask is how we can be sure we are in line with His perfect will. Sure, we can put the principles to practice, but how do we know His will on something for sure?

Let's match up the Scripture we just looked at with John 15:7. It says, *"If ye abide in Me, and My words abide in you, ye shall ask what ye will, and it shall be done unto you."* Here is our answer. We have to be dedicated to the things Jesus said, which we do by immersing ourselves in His Word. It really isn't some magical answer. It's a basic truth of Scripture. We need to put the Word of God into our hearts so much that it becomes so real to us that it actually causes our wills and God's will to become one.

The amazing thing is that when this happens we don't go through life feeling like obeying the will of God is some drudgery in which we have to turn our wills over, like giving up our dearest possessions. Yes, it involves that level of submission, but really what this Scripture reveals is that a transformation takes place inside us. Our wills transform into the will of God! In other words, the more Jesus' words are in our hearts, the more the things of God are important to us. Our priorities become more in line with the Lord's priorities.

This doesn't mean that you lose the simple, colorful things that make your personality unique, as if to become some kind of robot. You still have your preferences, hobbies, and personal likes and dislikes, just like I had with my preference for a house.

What transforms is every part of your will that is fleshly and carnal. When you dedicate yourself in God's Word, those carnal parts of your will diminish, and you begin to come into harmony with the will of God without even realizing it! You change and don't want the fleshly areas anymore. Then when you pray, you suddenly start to only ask God for things that are not self-motivated, but Bible-based. You suddenly don't have to second guess if God wants them for you; you just know!

Once you know God's will this way, you will have faith! You will pray with a different tone of voice. You will start to act like your prayers are complete, and you won't say things like, "Well God, if You want it…." No, you will pray like you know your request is going to come to pass. Something changes. Your will and God's will begin to match and become one, and it's not something you have to work at.

Another verse that repeats this truth is First John 3:22, which says, *"And whatsoever we ask, we receive of Him, because we keep His commandments, and do those things that are pleasing in His sight."* Why do we keep His commandments? It's because we are immersed in His Word. When God's words are in our hearts, we don't sin, compromise, and take on carnal beliefs.

When God's words abide in you, it's no longer a drudgery to follow Him. It becomes more natural. It feels less like obedience, even though obedience is involved, and more like something you have grown into.

In some ways, this is a key sign of spiritual maturity. It's like the difference between when your son is grown and has a family of his own, and when he was just a school-aged boy. After he has grown and has growing children of his own, he begins to appreciate the things his father provided for him as a child. The older he gets, the more he embraces his parents' virtuous values. You could say his maturity has caused his will to come more in line with his father's will. Greater harmony and agreement are the result.

As you follow these key principles, you will find yourself becoming more confident in your ability to hear and follow the will of God. I believe the Holy Spirit wants every Christian to live in this level of confidence. Then you will be able to move and operate with Him in harmony.

Lastly, I want to encourage you to tell the Lord how much you want to follow His will for your life. There is something about verbalizing it that causes you to be more committed in your own heart. That's why Jesus said, "Not My will, but Thine, be done" (see Luke 22:42). He was verbalizing it so He would reiterate to Himself the importance of following the will of God no matter what.

Talking to God about how much you want to obey Him causes His anointing to come and help you. Then even the areas of struggle in your life, where bad habits have taken hold and kept you from following God fully, will begin to melt in His hand. If there is some area in your heart where you are feeling resistant to turning something over to Him or releasing control, tell the Lord about it because He wants to help you work through it.

Isaiah 41:13 says, *"For I the Lord thy God will hold thy right hand, saying unto thee, Fear not; I will help thee."* God is there to help you in your weaknesses and to help you walk in His will for your life. Talk to Him and share your thoughts and feelings. You will open the way for the anointing to come in and change your heart, change circumstances, and move on your behalf.

I am amazed at how many things I have prayed about like this that have undergone a miraculous change in my heart. Things that had bothered me so badly in the past or frustrations I once had just melted away, and today I wonder why I even wasted time worrying over them. God can change your heart if you release it to Him and talk honestly with Him.

Sometimes we don't pray about something because we don't want to be honest with ourselves. It's OK; God knows it anyhow, and the more honestly we can talk to Him about where we are, the more He can help us change and conform to Him. The key is that we have to be willing to change and adjust and then know that He will do the rest.

My prayer is that you will feel a renewed sense of confidence today in locating God's will for your life and all the situations that concern you. You are probably more on track with God's plan for your life than you realize, and the roadmap to His divine direction is clearer than ever before. Yes, you are right where you need to be and confidently finding His perfect will for every situation!

About Brenda Kunneman

B renda Kunneman is cofounder of One Voice Ministries and with her husband pastors Lord of Hosts Church in Omaha, Nebraska. Brenda is a writer and teacher who ministers in many conferences and churches both nationally and internationally; preaching and demonstrating how to live life in the Spirit. Every day thousands visit her prophetic webpage called *The Daily Prophecy*. Through her ministry, many lives have been changed by accurate prophecies for individuals and churches. Brenda has authored several books, including *Decoding Hell's Propaganda, The Supernatural You,* and *When Your Life Has Been Tampered With.*

Other Books by Brenda Kunneman

The Supernatural You

When Your Life Has Been Tampered With

In the right hands, This Book will Change Lives!

Most of the people who need this message will not be looking for this book. To change their lives, you need to put a copy of this book in their hands.

> *But others (seeds) fell into good ground, and brought forth fruit, some a hundred-fold, some sixty-fold, some thirty-fold* (Matthew 13:8).

Our ministry is constantly seeking methods to find the good ground, the people who need this anointed message to change their lives. Will you help us reach these people?

> *Remember this—a farmer who plants only a few seeds will get a small crop. But the one who plants generously will get a generous crop* (2 Corinthians 9:6).

EXTEND THIS MINISTRY BY SOWING
3 BOOKS, 5 BOOKS, 10 BOOKS, OR MORE TODAY,
AND BECOME A LIFE CHANGER!

Thank you,

Don Nori Sr., Founder
Destiny Image
Since 1982

DESTINY IMAGE PUBLISHERS, INC.

*"Speaking to the Purposes of God for This Generation
and for the Generations to Come."*

VISIT OUR NEW SITE HOME AT
WWW.DESTINYIMAGE.COM

FREE SUBSCRIPTION TO DI NEWSLETTER

Receive free unpublished articles by top DI authors, exclusive

discounts, and free downloads from our best and newest books.

Visit www.destinyimage.com to subscribe.

Write to: Destiny Image
             P.O. Box 310
             Shippensburg, PA 17257-0310

Call: 1-800-722-6774

Email: orders@destinyimage.com

For a complete list of our titles or to place an order
online, visit www.destinyimage.com.

FIND US ON FACEBOOK OR FOLLOW US ON TWITTER.

www.facebook.com/destinyimage
www.twitter.com/destinyimage

Made in the USA
Columbia, SC
30 May 2020

98687400R00115